WINE DOGS

NEW ZEALAND

the dogs of New Zealand wineries

Craig McGill, Susan Elliott and Kevin Judd

A Giant Dog book

WINE DOGS NEW ZEALAND
THE DOGS OF NEW ZEALAND WINERIES

ISBN 978-1-921336-12-6

COPYRIGHT © GIANT DOG, FIRST EDITION 2008
WINE DOGS ® IS A REGISTERED TRADEMARK

DESIGNED BY SUSAN ELLIOTT, COPYRIGHT © McGILL DESIGN GROUP PTY LTD, 2008
ALL ILLUSTRATIONS COPYRIGHT © CRAIG McGILL, McGILL DESIGN GROUP PTY LTD, 2008
ALL TEXT NOT ATTRIBUTED, COPYRIGHT © CRAIG McGILL, McGILL DESIGN GROUP PTY LTD, 2008

ALL PHOTOGRAPHY © KEVIN JUDD, 2008 EXCEPT WHERE INDICATED

PRINTED BY APOL BOOKBUILDERS, CHINA
PROOFREADING AND EDITING BY VICKY FISHER

PUBLISHED BY GIANT DOG, ABN 27 110 894 178. PO BOX 964, ROZELLE NSW 2039 AUSTRALIA
TELEPHONE: (+612) 9555 4077 FACSIMILE: (+612) 9555 5985 INFO@WINEDOGS.COM
WEB: WWW.WINEDOGS.COM

FOR ORDERS: ORDERS@WINEDOGS.COM

OPINIONS EXPRESSED IN WINE DOGS ARE NOT NECESSARILY THOSE OF THE PUBLISHER.

OTHER TITLES BY CRAIG McGILL AND SUSAN ELLIOTT INCLUDE:
WINE DOGS AUSTRALIA – MORE DOGS FROM AUSTRALIAN WINERIES ISBN 978-1-921336-02-7
WINE DOGS DELUXE EDITION – THE DOGS OF AUSTRALASIAN WINERIES ISBN 0-9580856-2-5
WINE DOGS: USA EDITION – THE DOGS OF NORTH AMERICAN WINERIES ISBN 0-9580856-6-8
WINE DOGS USA 2 – MORE DOGS FROM NORTH AMERICAN WINERIES ISBN 978-1-921336-10-2
WINE DOGS ITALY / I CANI DEL VINO – I CANI DELLE AZIENDE VINICOLE ITALIANE ISBN 978-1-921336-11-9

HEALTH WARNING: VETERINARY ASSOCIATIONS ADVISE THAT EATING GRAPES, SULTANAS OR RAISINS CAN MAKE
A DOG EXTREMELY ILL AND COULD POSSIBLY RESULT IN FATAL KIDNEY FAILURE. IN THE INTERESTS OF CANINE
HEALTH AND WELLBEING, DO NOT FEED YOUR DOGS GRAPES OR ANY GRAPE BY-PRODUCT.

"*From the dog's point of view, his master is an elongated and abnormally cunning dog.*"

——— MABEL LOUISE ROBINSON

CONTENTS

ROVER

PET HATES: SHEEP AND COWS
FAVOURITE TOY: THE CAT'S BOWL
KNOWN ACCOMPLICE: MISSY THE CAT
FAVOURITE PASTIME: LYING IN THE SUN
OBSESSION: SITTING IN THE BACK OF UTES
FASTEST MEAL CONSUMED: STEAK OFF THE BBQ
NAUGHTIEST DEED: 5-LITRE URINATION ON THE CARPET

CLOUDY BAY MARLBOROUGH | BORDER COLLIE X, 14 | OWNERS: KEVIN AND KIMBERLEY JUDD

FOREWORD

by Kevin Judd

IT WAS SYDNEY 2003, pouring the new releases at Taste New Zealand, *a sea of eager wine trade pushing empty glasses in front of us, when out of the crowd pops up this long-haired Aussie with a big grin, "G'day mate, I love your photos, Craig McGill's the name and I'd like you to shoot some pictures for me in NZ"... Hmmmm, who is this bloke, should I know him?... "Yeah? I don't really do much commission work 'cause of the day job, what do you have in mind?" ... Perhaps he's the new art director for* Wine Magazine ..."I want you to photograph dogs for a book I am publishing" ... Dogs!? ... "You want me to do what? I'm no dog photographer"... "Yeah I know, but we want you to do it, it's called* Wine Dogs."*

Surely this guy was not in the wine trade, he must have snuck past the door minders, a book publisher, wine dogs, yeah right! This was not the first time I had heard such random ideas being floated towards the end of a big wine tasting!

Meanwhile, a sommelier was asking questions about the sustainability of Russian oak forests and a retailer was quizzing my colleague about her allocation of Te Koko ... "OK OK, I'll think about it, send me an email" ... assuming that was the last I'd hear from him, but it wasn't ...

My first attempt was a bit of a fluke really and gave me a soon-to-be-extinguished sense of confidence. Straight across the road at Allan Scott's, 'Billy', the neighbouring Jack Russell, was plonked on top of a barrel by his owner Josh, and there he sat willingly, flashing the occasional glance into the lens as I fired away. This is a piece of proverbial I thought, cruising down the road to pursue my second wine dog.

As I arrived at Forrest Estate a wire-haired terrier appeared from the cellar door wearing a green coat, complete with company branding – a hairy dog with invisible eyes that was clearly still being dressed by his parents. As friendly as he seemed, he had no interest in anything but the Pajero tyres and after a brief sniff retired to a basket in the back of the office. After a bit of verbal bullying by the staff, he was shuffled back outside where he proceeded to pay attention to everything except the camera, in fact he appeared to be intentionally ignoring me altogether.

"Patch, you're going to be famous! Sit boy, good boy, here, look, a biscuit, look at the man"; encouragement of all sorts was given by a small team of onlookers who had gathered around, and the volume and pitch slowly increased. More crackers were requisitioned from the smoko room and dangled in front of him, to which he

responded by turning his back. Arrrrghhh! His backside was returned to its previous position and bits of cheese were brought out to replace the dry biscuits ... so he rolled over onto his back.

I quickly realised that dogs are not the slightest bit interested in cameras and some even seem to suspect that they may have the potential to cause them great pain. There was the vineyard dog in Bannockburn that appeared to think the camera was a gun, and every time the shutter fired, it ran away, tail between the legs and ears back.

There was China the Shar Pei that looked as cuddly as that dog with the dunny rolls on TV. China nearly took a finger off when I tried to rearrange its pose in the front seat of a French military vehicle ... as you do.

And then there was Erik the Swedish Vallhund. Erik does not like men (as I discovered in retrospect) and he hates them even more when Michelle's not around. So, sneaking into the backyard when she was away was not the way to start a successful photo shoot. After an hour of tormenting Erik with bribes and threats, he had not remained still for one second and I reluctantly left empty-handed.

A second attempt was made, this time at the Peregrine winery with a female friend of Michelle's helping out. This attempt was equally dismal, obviously he remembered me and the things I had said in the backyard – once again, an hour or so was spent producing images of blurry fur.

But Erik had to be in the book, so he got another chance, this time in Marlborough with Michelle in attendance during a rather unorthodox photo session involving polished toe nails and a pinot noir fermentation, hmmmm...

Anyway, this time a silicon barrel bung was used to attract his attention and a long lens deployed to avoid his paranoia of close male proximity. Success at last after more than three hours in the making.

A hundred or so dogs later, at Gladstone Vineyard in the Wairarapa after a week on the road in the North Island, Baxter and Sophie seemed genuinely interested in my arrival. They did a few laps around the car sniffing and adding further complexity to the aroma that hundreds of kilometres of driving can never seem to budge. Once out of the car they followed behind me, noses in the air as if in a trance. They sat on command and stared intently into the lens, Baxter had slobber forming long trails from his jowls and was starting to blow bubbles by the time the roll of film had been exposed.

A round of applause for the two apparently obedient and obliging pooches erupted from a group of Wellingtonians enjoying a glass of pinot over in the garden. The sight of the two dogs sitting patiently side by side, staring attentively at the camera for ten minutes straight had the onlookers extremely impressed.

So what is the secret I hear you thinking "has this guy now got a thing going with dogs and learnt to communicate with them using dogs' body language?" No, this is no dog whisperer. In the words of Larry McKenna, after witnessing his dog Milo become spellbound from a close distance... "this is the Schmacko Man." Yes sir, the day I discovered Schmackos was the day it all became much easier. Baxter and Sophie were not behaving well for me, their owner or performing for the crowd, they were fixated by the piece of smelly, brown doggie treat that was protruding from the hand that was being used to focus the lens.

The dogs in this book regularly greet guests to their wineries, but they'll remember my visit as "the time this guy arrived in a 4WD that smelt like a kennel, teased and tormented me by holding up tasty treats and calling my name, put a shiny black thing in front of his face, whistled, told me I was a good dog, teased me again, made stupid dog noises, then finally threw me a Schmacko and drove off ... what was that all about?"

Despite the trials and tribulations, one of the greatest things about photographing dogs is their complete lack of ego or sense of self image, unlike some of their human companions. You can photograph a dog first thing in the morning or last thing at night, dribbling slobber, yawning, with their tongues hanging out, or scratching their arses (all of which winemakers are known to do frequently) and they couldn't care less.

You can publish these images and they don't take you to court, you can pat them on their backsides and give their ears a rub and they won't slap you. Dogs are bloody great to work with, so don't believe what they say about animals and children – you just need to be patient and have the odd trick or treat up your sleeve.

Thanks Craig and Sue! You sent me on a challenging mission and, although it took a coupla years longer than planned, I have thoroughly enjoyed it. Bring on the second edition!

KEVIN JUDD IS CHIEF WINEMAKER AT CLOUDY BAY VINEYARDS IN MARLBOROUGH, NEW ZEALAND AND IS ALSO ONE OF THE WORLD'S GREAT WINE PHOTOGRAPHERS. HIS VIBRANT VINEYARD LANDSCAPES OF NEW ZEALAND AND NUMEROUS OTHER COUNTRIES HAVE APPEARED IN MANY PUBLICATIONS AND EXHIBITIONS AROUND THE WORLD. AFTER PHOTOGRAPHING FOR *WINE DOGS*, HE ONLY HAS NINE FINGERS REMAINING. WWW.KEVINJUDD.CO.NZ

PET HATES:
FIREWORKS AND THUNDER
FAVOURITE PASTIME: SNEAKING OFF TO THE
MOA BREWERY FOR BEERS WHILE THE BOSS ISN'T LOOKING
NAUGHTIEST DEED: SNEAKING OFF TO THE
MOA BREWERY FOR BEERS WHILE THE BOSS ISN'T LOOKING

BUSTER

FAVOURITE TOY: PLASTIC BUCKETS
KNOWN ACCOMPLICE: KIPPER THE CAT
PET HATES: SHEEP, GETTING THE SACK FROM THE
SHEEP FARM, LARGE TRUCKS AND WINDSCREEN WIPERS
FAVOURITE PASTIME: SITTING IN THE PASSENGER'S SEAT
FAVOURITE FOODS: RABBITS AND INDIAN TAKEAWAY LEFTOVERS
NAUGHTIEST DEED: TAKING CLOTHES OFF THE LINE AND INTO THE PADDOCK

DIXIE

CLOUDY BAY VINEYARDS MARLBOROUGH | *BORDER COLLIE 'EYE DOG', 3* | *OWNERS: KEVIN AND KIMBERLEY TUD*

PET HATE: *BEING LEFT ALONE*
FAVOURITE PASTIME: *SUNBATHING*
FAVOURITE TOY: *STUFFED TOY DUCK*
NAUGHTIEST DEED: *THE 'WASN'T ME' POLICY*
KNOWN ACCOMPLICE: *CASPER THE FAMILY CAT*
FAVOURITE FOODS: *VINTAGE RABBIT AND POSSUM*

BRYNE

THOMAS

FAVOURITE PASTIME: LOOKING NERVOUS
NAUGHTIEST DEED: DOING NUMBER TWO IN THE OFFICE
PET HATE: BEING REMINDED OF THE OFFICE INCIDENT
FAVOURITE TOY: GERALD THE PRODUCTION MANAGER
OBSESSIONS: BLOWFLIES AND ELECTRIC BLANKETS

KNOWN ACCOMPLICE: BERT
OBSESSION: LICKING PEOPLE
PET HATE: BEING SHAMPOOED
FAVOURITE TOY: PLASTIC BOTTLES
FAVOURITE PASTIMES: CHASING CATS AND RABBITS
NAUGHTIEST DEED: EATING $4000 WORTH OF TUNNEL HOUSE WALL
FASTEST MEAL CONSUMED: PRUNER'S LUNCH, STILL IN THE WRAPPING

WALDO

BERT

PET HATE: HOSES
KNOWN ACCOMPLICE: WALDO
OBSESSION: PEEING ON CAR TYRES

PET HATE: WATER
FAVOURITE TOY: ANY SOCK
FAVOURITE FOOD: CAT FOOD
OBSESSION: CHASING THE CATS AWAY
KNOWN ACCOMPLICE: MAX THE SHEEP DOG
FAVOURITE PASTIME: SITTING ON GRANDDAD'S KNEE
NAUGHTIEST DEED: BARKING WHEN ON THE BACK OF THE UTE

MILO

OWNER: RAE

PET HATE: WATER

FAVOURITE PASTIME: EATING

*NAUGHTIEST DEED: EATING
THE BOTTLING GIRLS' LUNCHES*

*KNOWN ACCOMPLICES: ALEXANDER
AND WOLFGANG PUCK THE CAT*

FAVOURITE TOY: FOOD, MOMENTARILY

PET HATE: *BEING TIED UP*
FAVOURITE FOOD: *BABY RABBITS*
FAVOURITE TOY: *SHAGGY THE SOFT TOY*
NAUGHTIEST DEED: *CHEWING HORSES' TAILS*
FAVOURITE PASTIME: *CHASING FLIES AND MOTHS*
KNOWN ACCOMPLICE: *ASTRO THE YELLOW LABRADOR*

COOPER

MAXWELL

FAVOURITE TOYS: TENNIS BALL OR STICK
PET HATES: BIRD-SCARING SEASON AND CATS
KNOWN ACCOMPLICES: STELLA, PIP, LIBBY, CASE AND MONTY
FAVOURITE PASTIMES: SWIMMING AND DIVING
NAUGHTIEST DEED: INVOLVES A CAT – SAY NO MORE
FAVOURITE FOOD: TREATS FROM THE BOOT OF WINKIE'S CAR

STELLA AKA MRS FLUFFY

PET HATE: BEING LEFT BEHIND
FAVOURITE TOY: TENNIS BALL IN FLIGHT
FAVOURITE PASTIME: BEING THERE, JUST IN CASE
FAVOURITE FOOD: PLATE OF PORTERHOUSE STEAK
KNOWN ACCOMPLICES: MAX, PIP, LIBBY AND CASE
NAUGHTIEST DEED: EATING THE NEIGHBOUR'S CHOOK

OWNER: JAMES HEALY | BEARDED COLLIE, 3 | **DOG POINT VINEYARD** MARLBOROUGH | 21

OBAN

FAVOURITE PASTIME: SLEEPING
PET HATE: BIRD-SCARER BANGS
KNOWN ACCOMPLICE: CASHY BOY
FAVOURITE FOOD: SANDWICH TITBITS
NAUGHTIEST DEED: FLATULENCE IN THE TASTING LAB
(AND SHE KNOWS SHE'S IN TROUBLE WHEN SHE DOES IT)

FAVOURITE TOY: STICK
PET HATES: RAIN AND GUNS
FAVOURITE FOOD: ANYTHING
FAVOURITE PASTIME: SLEEPING
IN THE BACK OF THE TRUCK

CASH

DIANA

NAUGHTIEST DEED: CHEWING THE ARMCHAIR
OBSESSION: GERRY THE VINEYARD MANAGER
FAVOURITE PASTIME: GOING TO WORK AT THE VINEYARD
FAVOURITE TOY: THE DOGGIE TIMES, PLASTIC NEWSPAPER
KNOWN ACCOMPLICES: CHARLIE THE BLIND BICHON FRISE
FROM NEXT DOOR AND RATA CLIVE'S LABRADOR PUP
PET HATE: NOT GETTING TO LICK GERRY'S FACE IN THE MORNING

FAVOURITE TOY: TENNIS BALL
KNOWN ACCOMPLICE: BAXTER
NAUGHTIEST DEED: WEEING IN SOMEONE
ELSE'S BUCKETFUL OF WHITEBAIT AT THE RIVER
PET HATE: STAYING AT HOME WHEN MIKE AND DIANA GO OUT
FAVOURITE PASTIMES: RUNNING ALONGSIDE THE UTE AND EATING

LACHIE

SUMO

FAVOURITE TOYS: BUNGS AND BALLS
FAVOURITE PASTIME: CHASING WILD PIGS
NAUGHTIEST DEED: CHEWING IRRIGATION
DRIPPERS AND PLAYING IN THE RESULTING POOL
KNOWN ACCOMPLICES: SPARK, SALLY AND NIMO
FAVOURITE FOOD: SCRAMBLED EGGS WITH EXTRA MILK
PET HATE: YOUNG PUPS ANNOYING HIM WHILE SUNBAKING

NAUGHTIEST DEED: PULLING CLOTHES FROM
OFF THE LINE AND STASHING THEM IN HIS KENNEL
PET HATE: THE FOUR-WHEELER – HE BITES THE TYRES
FAVOURITE TOY: SHOES STOLEN FROM THE BACK DOOR
KNOWN ACCOMPLICES: STONE AND RED, HIS BROTHERS
FAVOURITE FOOD: WEETBIX WITH LOTS OF MILK AND EGGS ON TOP
FAVOURITE PASTIMES: CHASING DUCKS AND TEARING TENNIS BALLS APART

FOX

KRUZ (FRONT)

OBSESSION: FOOD
KNOWN ACCOMPLICE: KAHN
FAVOURITE TOY: OLD VOLLEY BALL
FAVOURITE FOOD: RAW RED MEAT
PET HATE: NOT GOING TO THE VINEYARD
NAUGHTIEST DEED: BREAKING TWO POTS AND
SPREADING THREE PALM TREES ON THE LAWN
FAVOURITE PASTIME: SPENDING TIME IN THE VINEYARD

FAVOURITE FOOD: BACON
KNOWN ACCOMPLICE: KRUZ
FAVOURITE PASTIME: SLEEPING
PET HATE: BEING SENT OUTSIDE
OBSESSION: PEOPLE'S ATTENTION
FAVOURITE TOY: OLD BIKE TYRE HANGING FROM A TREE
NAUGHTIEST DEED: JUMPING OUT OF THE CANOPY WINDOW
OF A MOVING VEHICLE AND DISAPPEARING FOR THREE DAYS

OBSESSION: SHADOWS
KNOWN ACCOMPLICE: BONNIE
PET HATE: NOT COMING TO WORK
FAVOURITE TOYS: DEAD RABBITS AND HARES
FAVOURITE FOOD: ANYTHING BUT RAW CARROTS
FAVOURITE PASTIME: CATCHING RABBITS AND HARES
NAUGHTIEST DEED: STEALING A DOZEN HOT CROSS BUNS

MOBY

CROCUS

PET HATE: PESKY PUKEKO

FAVOURITE FOOD: THE DOGGIE TREATS
WINERY STAFF BRING FOR HER MORNING TEA

OBSESSION: TO RID THE WORLD OF PESKY PUKEKO

NAUGHTIEST DEED: EATING AUNTY JANNE'S FAMOUS
SPONGE KISSES IN THE CAR EN ROUTE TO A LUNCHEON

FAVOURITE PASTIMES: COURTING CUSTOMERS FOR
ATTENTION AND PRACTISING HER WIDE-TOOTHED SMILE

KNOWN ACCOMPLICE: MIKO THE 18-YEAR-OLD BURMESE CAT

PET HATE: SKATEBOARDERS
FAVOURITE PASTIMES: STEALING
FOOD AND ROLLING IN POO
FAVOURITE FOOD: ANYTHING GAINED ILLICITLY
FAVOURITE TOY: SHEEP, A CHILD'S STUFFED TOY
KNOWN ACCOMPLICE: EDMUND THE SPHYNX CAT
NAUGHTIEST DEED: JUMPING UP ON THE MANAGING
DIRECTOR'S DESK AND STEALING HIS LUNCH

GUIDO

OWNER: SIMON NUNNS | ITALIAN GREYHOUND, 2 | COOPERS CREEK VINEYARD, AUCKLAND

31

KNOWN ACCOMPLICE: CP
PET HATE: MOUTHWASH
FAVOURITE TOY: RUGBY BALL
OBSESSIONS: STICKS AND BALLS
FAVOURITE FOOD: ANYTHING WITH CARROTS IN IT
FAVOURITE PASTIMES: SLEEPING AND CHASING STICKS

ALF

MOUNTFORD VINEYARD NORTH CANTERBURY | LABRADOR, 9 | OWNER: CP LIN

DOGS AND WINE
AND THOUGHTS IN BETWEEN

by CP Lin

FROM THE DAWN OF HUMANITY, two unbreakable opposing forces have governed and shaped our lives. On one side is the instinct to survive, procreate and pass on the genetic blueprint, and on the other is a desire to be super-human. This desire is driven by imagination, creativity and philosophy. To put it another way, the opposing forces are existence and transcendence; the human being and the imagined god. To stop us from being torn apart by these forces, some of us have searched for solutions over the millennia.

This conflict, if not resolved, or at least kept in check, can have disastrous consequences. If one chooses existence, one becomes a victim of mediocrity, living from day to day with nothing to say. If one chooses transcendence, the cerebral overload can result in self destruction: the fate of many past dictators.

And if one chooses the middle ground, one might be left in limbo with nowhere to go.

My contention for the best solution to this dilemma is to bridge the polar opposites and strive for a peaceful and enjoyable life. Dogs and wine can be two of these bridges. Dogs and wine fire the imagination within and encapsulate the nature around us.

Our wish to go beyond our physical abilities led us to invent tools: fire and a sharp edge, and to befriend animals that possess qualities we lack, for example, horses for transport and oxen to plough the fields and so on. Among those tamed animals, the dog fulfils most of our expectations. With its unfailing loyalty, its superior senses, its steadfast obedience and its desire to please, the dog, from its wolfish ancestors to the toy Pekinese, is truly our best friend. All it asks for is our companionship, leadership and inclusion in our society. This symbiotic relationship gives us human and super-human qualities in one package.

To quote Hugh Johnson, wine has the power to banish care. For millennia humans who have tasted wine believe that they are being given a preview of paradise. For a while, under its effect, they felt like god. Wine has been the preferred drink of philosophers since its discovery. It makes ideas flow easier, lessens inhibition and banishes care. Yet for all its super-human qualities, it requires all human attention to grow and make this divine drink.

As one can see from this brief discussion, dogs and wine are richly intertwined with our lives. They bridge the gap between human and the desire to be super human: thereby making our existence bearable.

CP LIN IS THE WINEMAKER FOR MOUNTFORD ESTATE IN NEW ZEALAND AND A CONSULTANT FOR WHOEVER NEEDS HIS SKILLS TO BUILD A FINE WINE. MOST OF THE TIME CP IS ACCOMPANIED BY ALF, HIS SEEING-EYE DOG.

KNOWN ACCOMPLICE: ALF
PET HATE: THE VACUUM CLEANER
FAVOURITE FOOD: HIGH-QUALITY STEAK
OBSESSION: SORTING OUT THE RABBITS
NAUGHTIEST DEED: ROLLING IN COW POO
FAVOURITE PASTIME: FOLLOWING
BUFFY AROUND THE HILLSIDE PROPERTY

JESS

GROWLER

OBSESSIONS: CATS AND RABBITS
PET HATE: BEING PHOTOGRAPHED
FAVOURITE BOOK: THE CAT IN THE HAT
FASTEST MEAL CONSUMED: PAN-FRIED PORK WITH HONEY GLAZE
FAVOURITE PASTIME: TREMBLING OUTSIDE THE WINDOW IN VIEW OF DINING PUNTERS

FAVOURITE PASTIME: RUNNING TO THE VINEYARD
FAVOURITE TOY: ANYTHING THAT SQUEAKS
PET HATE: OUR NEIGHBOUR GRAHAM CROFT
OBSESSION: BOTTOMS OF LARGE
MIDDLE-AGED WOMEN IN TIGHT TROUSERS
NAUGHTIEST DEED: BITING FIVE OF THE
ABOVE DURING HER ADOLESCENCE

RIEUSSEC

FAVOURITE PASTIMES: SWIMMING IN THE
RIVER AND CHASING RABBITS IN THE VINEYARD.
PET HATES: WET WEATHER AND BEING TIED UP.
FAVOURITE FOOD: SCHMACKOS REAL BEEF STRIPS
FAVOURITE TOY: ANY STICK PICKED UP AT THE RIVER
KNOWN ACCOMPLICE: TAWA THE BORDER COLLIE CROSS
NAUGHTIEST DEED: CHASING A LOCAL FARMER'S SHEEP ACROSS COUNTRY

JESS

PET HATE: BEING CHAINED UP
KNOWN ACCOMPLICE: FLASH THE CAT
FAVOURITE PASTIME: ESCAPING OUT OF THE FRONT
DOOR AND RUNNING AROUND THE NEIGHBOURHOOD
NAUGHTIEST DEED: BEING BROUGHT HOME BY THE
RANGER AFTER EATING A LOCAL FARMER'S CHICKENS
FAVOURITE FOOD: ANYTHING OTHER THAN DOG BISCUITS

FRED

OWNER: GORDON RUSSELL | DALMATIAN, 8 | **ESK VALLEY ESTATE** HAWKES BAY

ASH

FAVOURITE FOOD: TUX BISCUITS
FAVOURITE TOY: OLD YELLOW BALL
PET HATE: THE BIRD-SCARING SHOTGUN
NAUGHTIEST DEED: BARKING AT THE MOTORBIKE
KNOWN ACCOMPLICE: PENNY FROM FELTON ROAD
FAVOURITE PASTIMES: SWIMMING AND PLAYING WITH HER BALL

CORNISH POINT CENTRAL OTAGO | BLUE HEELER X, 7 | OWNERS: CRAIG AND LEANNE WHEELER

FAVOURITE FOOD: BUNNY
FAVOURITE TOY: TENNIS BALL
KNOWN ACCOMPLICE: ASH FROM CORNISH POINT
PET HATE: JANCIS THE CAT, JANCIS THE CAT, JANCIS THE CAT...
FAVOURITE PASTIMES: ROUNDING UP THE VINEYARD CHICKENS
AND KEEPING A SAFE DISTANCE FROM JANCIS THE WINERY CAT
NAUGHTIEST DEED: SPINNING 360 DEGREES IN THE BACK OF MUM'S CAR

PENNY

HUNTER

FAVOURITE PASTIME: EATING
FAVOURITE TOY: HIS STASH OF TENNIS BALLS
NAUGHTIEST DEED: STEALING A PAIR OF VERY
EXPENSIVE SHOES AND CHEWING THEM TO BITS
FAVOURITE FOOD: ANYTHING AND EVERYTHING
KNOWN ACCOMPLICE: SASHA THE BLACK LABRADOR
PET HATE: BEING PUT OUT IN HIS KENNEL ON COLD WINTER NIGHTS

FAVOURITE TOY: BUNGS
FAVOURITE FOODS: BUNGS AND BACON
FAVOURITE PASTIME: FINDING, FETCHING,
STEALING AND MAKING PILES OF BUNGS
PET HATE: HAVING BUNGS CONFISCATED
KNOWN ACCOMPLICES: ALEXIS, CARLOS AND LARS
NAUGHTIEST DEED: STEALING BUNGS FROM FULL BARRELS

GEMMA

PET HATE: THE GEESE
FAVOURITE TOY: THE GEESE
NAUGHTIEST DEED: CHASING CHOOKS
FASTEST MEAL CONSUMED: A WORKER'S LUNCH
KNOWN ACCOMPLICES: JACKSON AND ELIZA MATTHEWS
FAVOURITE PASTIME: CHASING GIRL DOGS
FAVOURITE MOVIE: A FISH CALLED WANDA

SCOTT

SPENCER

OBSESSION: EATING INNER SOLES
FAVOURITE FOOD: BAKED CHICKEN
FAVOURITE PASTIME: CHASING COOPER
FAVOURITE TOY: ANYTHING COOPER HAS
NAUGHTIEST DEED: PEEING ON THE X-BOX
KNOWN ACCOMPLICES: COOPER AND ELIZA
PET HATE: MISSING OUT ON GOING TO THE FARM

OBSESSION: PUSHING IN FOR A PAT
FAVOURITE FOODS: MEAT AND MORE FOOD
NAUGHTIEST DEED: PLAYING WITH A DEAD EEL
PET HATE: WHEN JACKSON BLOWS IN HIS FACE
KNOWN ACCOMPLICES: SPENCER AND JACKSON
FAVOURITE TOY: ANYTHING HE CAN GET OFF SPENCER
FAVOURITE PASTIMES: GOING TO THE FARM AND RUNNING

COOPER

OWNERS: ELIZA AND JACKSON MATTHEWS | BICHON FRISE, 1 AND LABRADOR, 2 | **RIVERBY ESTATE** MARLBOROUGH   45

GAJA III

PET HATE: THE CAT
FAVOURITE TOY: SOCCER BALL
OBSESSION: MURDERING SOCCER BALLS
NAUGHTIEST DEED: TO BE ANNOUNCED!

FROMM WINERY MARLBOROUGH │ BORDER COLLIE X, 7 WEEKS │ OWNERS: HATSCH AND SIMON KALBERER, LAVINIA HTROK

FAVOURITE TOY: THE CAT
FAVOURITE FOOD: MEAT
NAUGHTIEST DEED: CHASING THE CAT
FAVOURITE PASTIME: CHASING THE CAT
PET HATES: LOUD NOISES AND BEING TOLD OFF
KNOWN ACCOMPLICE: SAUSAGE THE DACHSHUND

HOOVER

PIPI

PET HATE: CATS
OBSESSION: FOOD
FAVOURITE TOYS: ALL THE CHILDRENS'
FAVOURITE PASTIME: GOING HORSE RIDING
NAUGHTIEST DEED: EATING FOOD FROM OFF THE BENCH
KNOWN ACCOMPLICES: ARCHIE, FLOYD AND THE HORSES
FAVOURITE FOOD: ANYTHING, ESPECIALLY IF IT'S ON THE BENCH

PET HATE: CATS
FAVOURITE TOY: FOOD
OBSESSION: OPOSSUMS
FAVOURITE PASTIME: SLEEPING
FAVOURITE FOOD: EVERYTHING
KNOWN ACCOMPLICES: PIPI, OSCAR AND FLOYD
NAUGHTIEST DEED: SLEEPING ON THE BED WHEN WET

TAFFY

FAVOURITE TOY: JACK
FAVOURITE FOOD: PEOPLE FOOD
NAUGHTIEST DEED: LEAVING THE PROPERTY
AND STAYING AWAY FOR THREE DAYS OR SO
PET HATE: NOT BEING ALLOWED TO SIT IN LAPS
FAVOURITE PASTIMES: DIGGING HOLES AND RABBITING
OBSESSION: GUARDING THE PROPERTY FROM INTRUDING DOGS

BELLA

PET HATE: *BEING GROWLED AT*
FAVOURITE TOY: *PURPLE STUFFED LION*
NAUGHTIEST DEED: *LEAVING THE PROPERTY AND STAYING AWAY FOR THREE DAYS OR SO*
OBSESSIONS: *OPENING DOORS AND GREETING GUESTS WITH A CUDDLY BLANKET IN HIS MOUTH*
FAVOURITE PASTIMES: *DIGGING HOLES AND RABBITTING*
FAVOURITE FOODS: *CHICKEN SCRAPS, VEGETABLES AND GRAVY*

JACK

NICO

KNOWN ACCOMPLICE: *HEIDI THE CAT*
FAVOURITE FOOD: *ANYTHING ON A BONE*
NAUGHTIEST DEED: *PRETTY GOOD HOLE DIGGER*
FAVOURITE PASTIMES: *SURVEYING HIS SURROUNDINGS TO ENSURE ALL IS WELL AND CHECKING ON THE CHILDREN*
PET HATE: *CHICKENS TRYING TO EAT HIS DOG BISCUITS*

PET HATES: FIREWORKS, HOUSEFIRES,
AMERICANS AND BEING AWAY FROM MATT
FAVOURITE FOODS: FOIE GRAS AND DUCKS
NAUGHTIEST DEED: EATING LIVE DUCKLINGS
FAVOURITE TOY: THE INDESTRUCTIBLE SPEAKER BONE
KNOWN ACCOMPLICES: ZEPHYR, TRICKS, MILLY AND BALLS
FAVOURITE PASTIMES: BALLS, RABBITS AND MORNING SNUGGLES

ECHO

OWNER: MATT EVANS | LABRADOR X, 7 | **DE VINE WINES** CENTRAL OTAGO | 53

NORTON

PET HATE: VET VISITS
FAVOURITE PASTIME: THE BEACH
KNOWN ACCOMPLICE: MORRIS THE CAT
FAVOURITE FOODS: SIRLOIN STEAK AND SMOKED SALMON
NAUGHTIEST DEED: EATING A PACKET OF RAT POISON AND BEING TREATED FOR IT

STONYRIDGE VINEYARD WAIHEKE ISLAND | LABRADOR, 10 | OWNER: STEPHEN WHITE

PET HATE: SKATEBOARDS
FAVOURITE TOY: GARY'S SOCKS
FAVOURITE PASTIME: BEACHTIME
OBSESSION: BURYING STONES IN THE SAND
NAUGHTIEST DEED: WALKING ON THE NEW WINERY SIKAFLOOR
KNOWN ACCOMPLICE: THE RUBBISH SACK-TEARING BLACK LAB
FAVOURITE FOOD: WHATEVER HE CAN GET WITHIN ONE METRE OF HIS MOUTH

CHARLIE

PET HATE: FENCES
FAVOURITE TOY: BALLS
FAVOURITE FOOD: MEAT BONES
KNOWN ACCOMPLICES: ALL THE VINEYARD STAFF
NAUGHTIEST DEED: POOING ON THE WINERY FRONT LAWN
FAVOURITE PASTIMES: ATV RIDING, HUNTING BIRDS AND SOCIALISING

MILO

FAVOURITE TOY: SOGGY OLD BONE
PET HATE: BEING LEFT IN HIS KENNEL
FAVOURITE FOOD: WHATEVER THE PIG IS HAVING
NAUGHTIEST DEED: CHEWING SHOES, WETSUITS AND EARMUFFS
KNOWN ACCOMPLICES: HENRY, BRUNO, MONTY AND TED THE PIG
FAVOURITE PASTIMES: CHASING RABBITS AND SNORING BY THE FIRE

PUKA

PET HATE: VINEYARD MOTORBIKE
KNOWN ACCOMPLICES: ALL THE FARM DOGS
FAVOURITE TOYS: FEATHER DUSTER AND TOILET ROLLS
NAUGHTIEST DEED: STEAMING PILE IN THE WINERY DOORWAY
FAVOURITE FOOD: LAMB SHANKS – BURIED AND DUG UP TWICE
FAVOURITE PASTIMES: BARKING AT HEDGEHOGS AND STAYING WARM

KIP

OBSESSION: CHASING CARS
PET HATE: THE BOSS'S BOOT
KNOWN ACCOMPLICE: MAVERICK THE CAT
NAUGHTIEST DEED: DOING BOMBS IN THE OFFICE
FAVOURITE PASTIME: SLEEPING ON HIS BEANBAG
FASTEST MEAL CONSUMED: ALL FOOD ESPECIALLY CHOCOLATE

PATCH

FIRE

OBSESSION: RABBITS
FAVOURITE PASTIME: WALKS
PET HATES: GUNS AND FIREWORKS
FAVOURITE TOY: ANYTHING THAT CAN BE THROWN AND RETRIEVED
NAUGHTIEST DEED: EATING A FAIR BIT OF THE FRONT OF SAM'S MINI –
MOTIVE UNKNOWN, POSSIBLY PROMPTED BY RABBIT
KNOWN ACCOMPLICE: GRACE, A SHEEPDOG SADLY BAFFLED BY SHEEP

MY DOG CAN LIP-READ

by Sam Neill

NOT THAT SHE'S SMARTER THAN OTHER DOGS. Smart enough though. It's just that now she's stone deaf, poor old thing. So when it's time for a walk, I come up behind her, tap her on the shoulder; she turns around and looks at me intently and I mouth silently the magic word W-A-L-K. In a heartbeat she jumps up and rockets out the door.

When I say, old, she's probably very old, but we're not quite sure how old, exactly. She's a rescue dog. When we found her, she was starving and much neglected. We took her on temporarily while we waited for her owner to get better. In those few weeks she so quickly worked her way into our family, and into our hearts, that we couldn't bear to part with her. With luck, the owner decided she was better off with us, and she's now been central to our lives for about ten years. Now we dread the day when she finally dies. Unthinkable.

One thing we know for sure is we couldn't now own another breed. I get incensed when I read Staffordshire Bull Terriers lumped in with "dangerous breeds" in the press. While she doesn't tolerate nonsense from other dogs, Fire couldn't be a more gentle creature with people, and in particular small children. Even now, in her old age, she loves to play with kids. And with oldies like me.

She's everything you could want from a dog: loyal, patient, friendly, loving and the best company. Everywhere I go, she insists she goes too. But when I go overseas to work she has to stay behind. This breaks her little heart. And mine. Just the sight of a suitcase, and she slumps into despair. Nowadays, I use all kinds of tricks to try and conceal my departure, but somehow, a day or two in advance, she knows, and I see her getting sad. Still, she's a resilient and cheerful dog and she soon settles into the manager's house on the vineyard. I've made her a kennel there (heated for god's sake, as a salve to my conscience). She hasn't used it once; she prefers to sleep with the kids. Who can blame her? And anyway she's always been a part-time nanny.

PHOTOGRAPH © BOB CAMPBELL 2008

Ironically her deafness has turned out to be something of a blessing. For years any kind of a bang would send her into a tail-spin and under the table. Guns, fireworks, thunder: all a source of terror. This is tricky if you're a farm dog, which she now is. Now, however, she sails happily through the vineyard and the orchard at duck-shooting time, or while bird-scaring is at its zenith, not a care in the world.

She's only ever had one job, and a job she took very seriously indeed: rabbit control. To my knowledge, I think she only caught one, ever – and that was very small indeed. And probably a bit thick. Still, every time she got a chase on, she couldn't have enjoyed herself more.

We hope we've still got a few more years of rabbiting to go. Fingers, and paws, crossed. And here's another word she can lip-read: R-A-B-B-I-T!

SAM NEILL IS AN ITINERANT ACTOR WHO HAS A LONGSTANDING INTEREST IN WINE, PARTICULARLY RED WINE, WHICH ACCOUNTS FOR HIS RUDE GOOD HEALTH. HE IS VERY PROUD OF EVERYTHING ABOUT TWO PADDOCKS, AND WILL BORE YOU TO DEATH ON THE SUBJECT IF YOU GIVE HIM A CHANCE. DON'T. SAM HAS VISIONS OF A VAST TWO PADDOCKS EMPIRE, BUT IS USUALLY BETTER THE NEXT DAY. HE PLAYS CRICKET BADLY AND ALSO THE UKULELE. PRETENDS TO BE A FLY FISHERMAN AND IS NOT RELATED TO SAM HUNT. HELPS PROVIDE FOCUS FOR THE TALENTS OF NEW ZEALAND AND AUSTRALIAN FILMMAKERS (SEE HUNTAWAY FILMS). SAM IS AN ACTIVE PROPONENT OF PROTECTING AND PRESERVING NEW ZEALAND'S PRECIOUS NATURAL RESOURCES. HE IS A MEMBER OF THE *SUSTAINABILITY COUNCIL OF NEW ZEALAND*, A TRUSTEE OF THE *NATIONAL PARKS AND CONSERVATION FOUNDATION* AND A PATRON FOR *WAITAKI FIRST*. PHOTO OF FIRE (PAGE 60) © GILBERT VAN REENEN 2008. PHOTO OF SAM AND FIRE (PAGE 62) © BOB CAMPBELL 2008.

PET HATE: PEOPLE WHO IGNORE HER
FAVOURITE PASTIME: SLEEPING IN THE UTE
KNOWN ACCOMPLICE: HER BROTHER CHOPIN
OBSESSION: CHASING WILD CATS AND RABBITS
FASTEST MEAL CONSUMED: STOLEN BBQ SAUSAGES
FAVOURITE TOYS: STUFFED RABBIT AND A SQUASH BALL
NAUGHTIEST DEED: HELPING HERSELF TO BBQ SAUSAGES

BLISS

DAYNA

FAVOURITE TOY: SOFT TOYS
KNOWN ACCOMPLICE: BUDDY
FAVOURITE PASTIME: STALKING KATHRYN
NAUGHTIEST DEED: RUBBING HERSELF ON SOFT TOYS
FAVOURITE FOOD: ANYTHING SUITABLE FOR HUMAN CONSUMPTION
PET HATE: BEING SHUT UP AND UNABLE TO GET OUT ON THE VINEYARD WITH KATHRYN

ASKERNE HAWKES BAY | JACK RUSSELL TERRIER, 3 | OWNERS: JOHN AND KATHRYN LOUGHLIN

PET HATE: WATER
FAVOURITE FOOD: A LARGE JUICY BONE
KNOWN ACCOMPLICES: DAYNA AND LILLY
NAUGHTIEST DEED: URINATING ON A JEHOVAH'S WITNESS VISITOR
FAVOURITE PASTIMES: GOING FOR A WALK AND CATCHING BIRDS IN NETS

BUDDY

HARRY

FAVOURITE TOY: OTHER DOGS
FAVOURITE PASTIME: MAKING TROUBLE
KNOWN ACCOMPLICES: MOLLY AND LUCY
PET HATE: BEING SHUT IN ON A WET DAY
NAUGHTIEST DEED: TOO MANY TO MENTION
FAVOURITE FOOD: ANYTHING EXCEPT LETTUCE AND CUCUMBER

KNOWN ACCOMPLICE: ALBERTO
FAVOURITE PASTIMES: EATING AND
GOING WALKABOUT (IF NO ONE IS LOOKING)
NAUGHTIEST DEED: GOING WALKABOUT
FAVOURITE FOOD: ANYTHING AND EVERYTHING
PET HATES: THE CHAIN AND THE DREADED DIET MENU

JOVI

MOLLY

FAVOURITE PASTIME: EATING
FAVOURITE TOY: SOFT SQUEAKY MALLARD DUCK
NAUGHTIEST DEED: EATING ALL THE FINGER FOOD AT AN EVENT
PET HATE: FEEDING TIME FOR ANYONE OTHER THAN HERSELF
KNOWN ACCOMPLICES: WINNIE SINCLAIR-THOMSON AND TRUFFLE WALDING

FAVOURITE TOY: TENNIS BALLS
FAVOURITE FOOD: FRESH EGGS
PET HATE: SMALL FOOD PORTIONS
NAUGHTIEST DEED: SNIFFING A CHICKEN TO DEATH
FAVOURITE PASTIME: DISCIPLINING THE CATS AT HOME
OBSESSIONS: POSSUMS UP TREES AND RABBITS IN VINEYARD
KNOWN ACCOMPLICES: FAT BASTARD AND RAMSES THE CATS

COCO

STORM

FAVOURITE PASTIME: SLEEPING
FAVOURITE FOOD: BIG BONES
FAVOURITE TOY: COKE BOTTLE
NAUGHTIEST DEED: BARKING AT A BIRD AT 2AM

FAVOURITE TOY: HIS CUDDLY RUG
FAVOURITE PASTIME: LYING IN THE SUN
KNOWN ACCOMPLICE: ANNABEL THE GOAT
OBSESSION: GETTING TO HIS FAVOURITE MAT
NAUGHTIEST DEED: CHASING SHEEP WITH INTENT
FAVOURITE FOOD: GOURMET FOOD FROM THE CAFÉ
PET HATE: NOT BEING ALLOWED TO SLEEP ON THE WHITE LOUNGE SOFAS

DHARMA

DAISY

FAVOURITE PASTIME: SLEEPING
FAVOURITE FOOD: THE CAT'S FOOD
FAVOURITE TOY: A RUBBER BARBELL
PET HATE: PEOPLE TALKING TO CHRISTINE THROUGH
THE CAR WINDOW – ESPECIALLY TRAFFIC OFFICERS
NAUGHTIEST DEED: EATING A WHOLE BAR OF DARK CHOCOLATE
AND GINGER, THEN THROWING UP ON CHRISTINE'S BED

FAVOURITE FOOD: ANYTHING KIM IS EATING
KNOWN ACCOMPLICES: QUEENIE AND KAS
NAUGHTIEST DEED: RUNNING AWAY FROM
HOME AND ALL THE WAY TO THE OFFICE (4KM)
FAVOURITE TOY: ANYTHING QUEENIE IS PLAYING WITH
PET HATES: KIM GOING AWAY, COURIERS AND FIREWORKS
FAVOURITE PASTIME: FOLLOWING KIM AROUND IN BETWEEN NAPS

SPOOKY

BUDDY

NAUGHTIEST DEED: AMBUSHING HORSE RIDERS ALONG THE BOUNDARY FENCE (PRE-RETIREMENT)

FAVOURITE PASTIME: RACING PASSING DOGS ALONG THE BOUNDARY FENCE, MOSTLY IN HIS DREAMS

PET HATE: ANYTHING THAT INVOLVES WATER SPORTS

KNOWN ACCOMPLICE: DEARLY DEPARTED BELGIAN SHEPHERD MISHKA

PET HATE: BEING LEFT OUT IN THE COLD
FAVOURITE FOOD: ROAST DINNER BONES
OBSESSION: STEALING THE CHOOK'S FOOD
FAVOURITE TOY: ANYTHING FLUFFY, DEAD OR ALIVE
FAVOURITE PASTIME: SLIDING DOWN GRASSY SLOPES ON HIS BACK
NAUGHTIEST DEED: BITING HOLES IN VINE NETS, TRYING TO GET TO BIRDS

WILBUR

OWNERS: MARK HESSON AND DHANA PILLAI | LABRADOR X, 11 | LEANING ROCK VINEYARD, CENTRAL, OTAGO | 77

GOLDIE

PET HATE: MISSING A RUN
OBSESSION: HIS FRIEND RAFFERTY
KNOWN ACCOMPLICE: RAFFERTY LOVE
FAVOURITE TOY: OTHER PEOPLE'S SOCKS
FAVOURITE FOOD: VERY EXPENSIVE NUTS
NAUGHTIEST DEED: JUST BURYING ONE SOCK OF A PAIR
FAVOURITE PASTIME: BURYING OTHER PEOPLE'S SOCKS

FAVOURITE FOOD: TOTAL DOG SAUSAGE
KNOWN ACCOMPLICES: JACK AND RANGER
NAUGHTIEST DEED: JOINING IN KIDS' BALL GAMES, GRABBING THE BALL
AND PUNCTURING IT, BEFORE BRINGING IT HOME (SEVEN TIMES – COST $80)
FAVOURITE PASTIME: RIDING ON THE DUCK BOARD WHILE FISHING ON LAKE TAUPO
PET HATE: BEING LEFT BEHIND WHEN THE OTHER STOCK DOGS HEAD OFF FOR THE DAY

FELIX

FLASH

PET HATE: CATS
FAVOURITE TOY: CATS
KNOWN ACCOMPLICES: CELLAR RATS
FAVOURITE PASTIME: HIDING IN THE TRUCK
NAUGHTIEST DEED: SHE THINKS DUCK POO IS PERFUME

LIVINGSTONE

FAVOURITE TOY: *BUNNY RABBIT SOFT TOY*
PET HATES: *GARDEN HOSE AND VACUUM CLEANER*
FAVOURITE PASTIME: *MOVING BETWEEN SUN AND SHADE*
DURING SUMMER, SLEEPING BY THE FIRE DURING WINTER
FAVOURITE FOODS: *MEATY BITES WITH RICE AND CARROTS*
KNOWN ACCOMPLICE: *COCO THE SPRINGER SPANIEL FROM PORTERS PINOT*
NAUGHTIEST DEED: *CHEWING UP A QUAD BIKE SEAT AND OLD LOUNGE CHAIR*

FAVOURITE PASTIMES: RESTING IN THE BACK
OF THE UTE OR SLEEPING IN THE VINEYARD
FAVOURITE FOODS: SLOW RABBITS, SHELLED PINE NUTS AND CHEESE
PET HATES: BIRDS EATING HIS DOG ROLL AND SLEEPING OUTSIDE ON FROSTY NIGHTS

HUGO

OBSESSION: RABBITS
FAVOURITE TOY: TENNIS BALL
FAVOURITE PASTIME: HUNTING RABBITS
KNOWN ACCOMPLICE: FRIENDS FROM PONY CLUB
FAVOURITE FOOD: EYE FILLET STEAK – MEDIUM RARE
PET HATES: COLD FEET AND BEING USED AS A HOT-WATER BOTTLE
NAUGHTIEST DEED: POOING ON ROBYN'S DAUGHTER'S SCHOOL UNIFORM

SWEEP

PET HATE: CARS
FAVOURITE FOOD: EYE FILLET STEAK -BLUE
FAVOURITE PASTIME: CHEWING SWEEP'S BACK LEG
KNOWN ACCOMPLICES: DOT, WOODY, SLIPPER, HONEY, STAR AND POPPY
FAVOURITE TOY: HELLO HELLO, ROBYN'S DAUGHTER'S STUFFED TOY HORSE
NAUGHTIEST DEED: SPENDING 24 HOURS, LOST IN A HOLLOW TRUNK AFTER CLIMBING A TREE

WALTER

PET HATE: MISSING OUT
FAVOURITE FOOD: THE CATS'
KNOWN ACCOMPLICE: VAUGHAN
NAUGHTIEST DEED: ATTEMPTING
TO UNEARTH THE SEPTIC TANK
FAVOURITE PASTIME: ANYTHING ACTIVE
OBSESSION: BEING SOMEWHERE ELSE

JAZZ

OBSESSION: RABBITS
FAVOURITE FOOD: VENISON
FAVOURITE TOY: TOY RABBITS THAT SQUEAK
KNOWN ACCOMPLICES: FRIDAY AND NELSON
PET HATE: BAGS BEING PACKED FOR AN OVERSEAS TRIP
FAVOURITE PASTIMES: DIGGING UP RABBIT BURROWS AND WHITEBAITING

TONTO

FAVOURITE TOY: BROOM
FAVOURITE FOOD: POPCORN
OBSESSION: ENTITLEMENTS
NAUGHTIEST DEED: POO-ROLLING
PET HATE: PEOPLE ON HER COUCH
FAVOURITE PASTIME: SELF-CONGRATULATION
KNOWN ACCOMPLICE: BELLA (PICTURED AT BACK)

NINA

PET HATE: FROST
OBSESSION: SLEEP
FAVOURITE FOOD: POMACE
FAVOURITE TOY: CHICKENS
FAVOURITE PASTIME: SWIMMING
NAUGHTIEST DEED: SHOOT THINNING
KNOWN ACCOMPLICE: GINGER MEGS (300KG DUROC SOW)

TWIG

FAVOURITE TOY: FLAT RUGBY BALLS
PET HATE: EXPLOSIONS OF ANY KIND
OBSESSION: RUGBY BALLS, ESPECIALLY WHEN KICKED
FAVOURITE FOOD: ANYTHING EXCEPT BEANS AND BROCCOLI
NAUGHTIEST DEED: STAGE DIVING INTO A 10 TONNE PINOT FERMENT
KNOWN ACCOMPLICES: HIS BROTHERS KAPE, FIN, NIC AND DOMINGO THE CAT
FAVOURITE PASTIME: DREAMING ABOUT CHASING PARKED CARS

JASPA

*"I wonder what goes through his mind
when he sees us peeing in his water bowl."*

———— **PENNY WARD MOSER**

KATIE

PET HATE: *MORNING SPLASHES WITH COLD WATER*
OBSESSIONS: *FIRE, SPARKS, CLOTHING WITHIN GRABBABLE REACH*
FAVOURITE TOYS: *FIRE, SPARKS, CLOTHING WITHIN GRABBABLE REACH*
NAUGHTIEST DEED: *TEARING BRIDE'S BRAND NEW, NEXT-DAY $300 DRESS*
FAVOURITE FOOD: *SHOELACES (ATTACHED TO SHOE, ATTACHED TO PERSON)*
FAVOURITE PASTIME: *VOCAL CONTRIBUTIONS TO EARLY MORNING STAFF MEETINGS*

PET HATE: CATS
OBSESSION: BRETT
FAVOURITE TOY: BRETT
FAVOURITE FOOD: BONES
KNOWN ACCOMPLICES: PIPI, TINK, FLYNN AND PIXIE
NAUGHTIEST DEED: STEALING CARCASSES FROM BUTCHER
FAVOURITE PASTIME: SCHMOOZING TOURISTS AT THE VINEYARD

LOU

TINK

FAVOURITE FOOD: RABBIT
PET HATE: BIRDS IN VINE NETS
FAVOURITE TOY: CHARLIE'S SON FRED
OBSESSION: DIGGING RABBIT HOLES
KNOWN ACCOMPLICES: APRIL AND PIPI
NAUGHTIEST DEED: HAVING TO GET A TAXI HOME FROM SHOOTERS, THE LOCAL BAR
FAVOURITE PASTIMES: LONG WALKS IN THE COUNTRYSIDE AND AVALANCHE PATROLLING

FAVOURITE PASTIME: CHASING
TOSCA THE WINERY CAT (PICTURED)
FAVOURITE TOY: SQUEAKY DUCK-DUCK
NAUGHTIEST DEED: EATING THE STUFFING
OUT OF THE OFFICE CHAIR (ALSO PICTURED)
FAVOURITE FOOD: ANYTHING OFF THE SMOKO TABLE
KNOWN ACCOMPLICE: TOSCA THE BURMESE WINERY CAT
PET HATE: SLEEPING OUTSIDE AT NIGHT WHILE TOSCA STAYS IN

RUBY

PET HATE: BIRDS
FAVOURITE FOOD: RABBIT
FAVOURITE TOY: SOCCER BALL
NAUGHTIEST DEED: EATING GRAPES
FAVOURITE PASTIME: CHASING RABBITS

MURDOCH JAMES WAIRARAPA | BORDER COLLIE, 1 | OWNER: CARL FRASER

PET HATE: VACCINATION TIME
FAVOURITE TOY: THE NEIGHBOUR'S CATS
FAVOURITE FOOD: SPAGHETTI BOLOGNESE
FAVOURITE PASTIMES: GREETING FOLK AT CELLAR
DOOR AND DIGGING BIG HOLES IN THE GARDEN
KNOWN ACCOMPLICES: ROCCO AND GINGER THE CAT
NAUGHTIEST DEED: SCRATCHING AT THE CARPET UNTIL WORN THROUGH

PEPPER

LANCELOT

FAVOURITE TOY: SOCCER BALL
OBSESSION: RIDING THE QUAD BIKE
PET HATE: THE BOARDING KENNELS
KNOWN ACCOMPLICES: SWAN AND NAIK
FAVOURITE PASTIME: LEARNING A FOURTH LANGUAGE

OBSESSION: LOOKING FOR RABBITS
FAVOURITE TOY: STUFFED SHAR PEI
FAVOURITE TV CHANNEL: ANIMAL PLANET
PET HATES: HOME DETENTION AND VETS
KNOWN ACCOMPLICES: POLLY AND CLOVIS
FAVOURITE PASTIMES: SLEEPING AND DRESSING IN HUMAN CLOTHES
NAUGHTIEST DEED: INTIMIDATING NEIGHBOURHOOD SHEEP

CHINA

BINDI

FAVOURITE TOY: HARES
PET HATE: GETTING CLEAN
KNOWN ACCOMPLICE: FRAN
FAVOURITE PASTIME: SWIMMING
NAUGHTIEST DEED: STEALING MEAT FOR BBQ WITH FRAN

FAVOURITE TOY: HARES
PET HATE: GETTING CLEAN
KNOWN ACCOMPLICE: BINDI
FAVOURITE PASTIME: YELPING
NAUGHTIEST DEED: STEALING MEAT FOR BBQ WITH BINDI

FRAN

PUM PUM

PET HATE: KITTENS
FAVOURITE FOOD: BUNNIES
FAVOURITE TOY: BABY BUNNIES
FAVOURITE PASTIME: HUNTING BROWN FURRY THINGS
NAUGHTIEST DEED: DISPOSING OF THE CHRISTMAS KITTEN
KNOWN ACCOMPLICE: MADELEINE, HER 8-YEAR-OLD BOSS

FAVOURITE TOY: HAIRY THE CAT
FAVOURITE FOODS: MINCE AND CHEESE PIE
FAVOURITE PASTIMES: DIVING FOR ROCKS IN
THE RIVER AND FARTING IN CROWDED ROOMS
KNOWN ACCOMPLICES: DODGY BOB AND FAT BASTARD
PET HATES: RAIN AND BEING DRESSED BY PETER AND MAYI'S DAUGHTER
NAUGHTIEST DEED: JUMPING THROUGH OPEN WINDOW OF A SHAREHOLDER'S
CAR AND SLEEPING ON THE BACK SEAT AFTER SWIMMING IN THE RIVER

MISTER

OWNERS: PETER AND MAYI CALDWELL | STAFFORDSHIRE BULL TERRIER ♀ | TE KAIRANGA WAIRARAPA

MADDY

FAVOURITE TOY: RUBBER DUCK
NAUGHTIEST DEED: CHEWING SHOES
KNOWN ACCOMPLICES: OLLY THE CAT AND JUDE
FAVOURITE PASTIME: EXPLORING THE VINEYARD
WITH HIS MATE JUDE, THE VINEYARD MANAGER'S DOG

PET HATE: BURGLARS
OBSESSION: THE FOUR-WHEEL DRIVE
FAVOURITE TOY: SILICON CASK BUNGS
FAVOURITE FOOD: MEAT ON THE BONE
FAVOURITE PASTIME: PLAYING WITH WATER
NAUGHTIEST DEED: STEALING THREE T-BONE STEAKS

MAVERICK

KNOWN ACCOMPLICE: BELLA
FAVOURITE TOY: COOKIE MONSTER
OBSESSION: CHASING PARIS THE CAT
PET HATE: GETTING UP IN THE MORNING
NAUGHTIEST DEED: SNEAKING INTO THE FRIDGE AT NIGHT
FAVOURITE PASTIME: ANYTHING HE'S NOT ALLOWED TO DO
FASTEST MEAL CONSUMED: DINNER FOR FOUR, INCLUDING THE SALAD

BILLY

CHEZ JEF

by John Saker

THERE WAS NO JEF AND THERE WERE NO CATS when we came to live at the Villa Les Clos in the Provençal hamlet Le Flayosquet. The dominant living presence was Desirée Chevalier, our self-important landlady, who was installed in the upstairs flat. She was too awful to give a damn about animals, and too tight to feed one. Mme Chevalier redefined meanness for us one evening when she invited us to dinner at her place. At the end of it, she took out a piece of paper, added up the money she'd spent on the meal, magnanimously gave us small credit for the fine bottle of wine we'd brought, then asked for payment in cash before we left.

When the weather began to cool, Mme Chevalier moved back to her large apartment in Nice. The dust kicked up by her aged Peugeot bumping down the drive had hardly settled when the four-footed world began to mobilise, somehow knowing the coast was clear.

The cats came first. They had probably been living in the barn behind the house all the time. There was one we called Hunter because he or she was such a good one. Quick, tireless and – crucially – bloody hungry, Hunter would put on a compelling predatory display in the garden most afternoons. These cats were feral and untouchable, but they were still cats; hardwired to find and harvest affection. One of them would sit on our exterior kitchen windowsill in the evenings, twisting and preening with obvious pleasure as we stroked it – through the glass.

Jef bounded into our lives one morning when we were having breakfast on the terrace. Suddenly he was there, happy, panting, ready for anything. You knew straight away he was a good joker.

Hard to pin a breed on Jef; there were several in the mix. Brown and charcoal were his main colours, and his coat leaned towards shaggy. His border collie-like size and instincts pointed to a good dose of berger (sheep dog) of some kind. An elderly neighbour, la veuve Moulin, met us in the lane one day and told us his name. She identified a stone villa further along the olive tree-lined ridge from ours as being chez Jef.

Unlike the cats, his visits were not mainly about food. Jef loved to play, and in us he'd found willing playmates with some fun toys. The frisbee was a favourite. Jef would hold down one end of the small sloping field beside the villa. I'd drift the frisbee down towards him, and if it maintained a flight path about a metre and a half above his head, he'd take it every time. We used up a lot of film on Jef's acrobatic frisbee intercepts.

He shared his name with a wonderful, very emotional song by Jacques Brel. The song's simple, imploring chorus – viens Jef, viens – became our call to Jef. If he was lucky, he got a piece of verse as well.

The villa began to fill with friends arriving to stay and work the grape harvest. Jef wasn't complaining; more playmates meant more fun. He was at our place most of the time now, only disappearing at meal times. His owners obviously had faith. No-one ever came looking for him.

On the first day of the vendanges *Jef piled into the combi with all of us, probably thinking we were upping the canine entertainment stakes with a location shift. 'Il est marrant, ce chien' (that dog's a bit of dag) said Roger, the local farmer who had hired us to pick his grapes, observing Jef's crazed pursuit of birds or rabbits down the vine rows.*

But we were there to work, not play. We began labouring along the rows of squat bush vines, filling buckets with bunches of mediocre provençal Grenache, descending into a slow torture of lower back pain and self-inflicted secatur wounds. Jef hadn't anticipated this. For a while he wore a head-to-one-side mystified look. Then he produced some pissed-off sounding barks. We tossed him a few grapes. He ignored them. Sometime before noon, without anyone noticing, Jef was gone.

He was at the villa waiting at the end of the day and greeted us happily. But the renewed, hopeful wag soon left his tail as he watched us crawl from the combi – some bent double – into the villa to collapse. In one day we'd gone from being really bad sports to completely nul. Jef looked betrayed and disgusted. Though he lived surrounded by vineyards, he had serious shortcomings as a wine dog. For the second time that day Jef turned tail. He stayed away until the harvest was over and play could resume.

The following spring we married and had the wedding hoolie at the villa. Jef arrived during the afternoon to find a lot of old frisbee buddies and a horde of other likely prospects. He was in heaven, chasing Champagne corks and children around the property. Mme Chevalier tried to shoo him away but we felt entitled that day to overrule her.

Soon after the wedding, we left Le Flayosquet and Jef to live in London, but paid the hamlet one last visit before returning to New Zealand. We made the rounds of friends, neighbours, special places. No sign of Jef. So, for the first time, we went to his house. It was a strange thing, to knock on the door of a house, knowing nothing about the people who lived there, but asking for their dog by name. When Jef's head emerged from behind his puzzled owner's knee and gave us a heart-warming yelp of recognition, we laughed. When he led us outside and stood over a ball, our day was made. Jef was no kind of player when it came to making wine, but he was a player all right.

JOHN SAKER BEGAN WRITING ABOUT WINE IN 1998. BEFORE JOINING *CUISINE* MAGAZINE AS THE NEW ZEALAND WINE WRITER IN 2007 HE WAS A WEEKLY WINE COLUMNIST FOR AUCKLAND'S *WEEKEND HERALD*. HE IS THE AUTHOR OF TWO BOOKS, *TRACING THE ARC* AND *HOW TO DRINK A GLASS OF WINE*. HE IS CURRENTLY WORKING ON TWO WINE BOOKS: ONE ABOUT NEW ZEALAND PINOT NOIR, THE OTHER ABOUT WINE AND TRAVEL.

FAVOURITE FOOD: FISH AND CHIPS
PET HATES: THUNDER AND LIGHTNING
FAVOURITE PASTIME: ASSISTING WITH SECURITY
NAUGHTIEST DEED: DESTROYING UNATTENDED SHOES

THE CABBAGE TREE VINEYARD WAIRARAPA | AUSTRALIAN CATTLE DOG 12 WEEKS | OWNERS: DAVID AND WINIFRED BULL

FAVOURITE FOOD: FISH AND CHIPS
PET HATES: THUNDER AND LIGHTNING
FAVOURITE PASTIME: RABBIT AND BIRD CONTROL
NAUGHTIEST DEED: LEAPING THROUGH OPEN RESTAURANT
KITCHEN WINDOW IN THE MIDDLE OF CHEF'S PREP

RUBY

OSCAR

OBSESSION: COLLECTING CORKS
NAUGHTIEST DEED: BREAKING HIS LEG
KNOWN ACCOMPLICE: BEAVER THE BOXER
FAVOURITE PASTIME: GOING ANYWHERE IN THE CAR
FAVOURITE TOYS: A PURPLE BEAR AND 'GORILLA LEGS'
PET HATES: TRAILERS ATTACHED TO VEHICLES, UMBRELLAS AND RAINCOATS

REERUN DOVER

FAVOURITE PASTIME: SLEEPING
FAVOURITE TOYS: ROCKS AND BUNGS
FAVOURITE FOOD: BARBECUED ANYTHING
KNOWN ACCOMPLICES: MANU AND FOENIX
OBSESSION: DIGGING FOR ROCKS AT THE BEACH
NAUGHTIEST DEED: DEFECATION IN FRONT OF CELLAR DOOR
PET HATE: RETRIEVING STICKS FROM FAST-FLOWING RIVERS IN WINTER

WILLOW

FAVOURITE TOY: STONES
NAUGHTIEST DEED: EATING STONES
FAVOURITE PASTIME: CHASING RABBITS
OBSESSION: CARRYING STONES IN HER MOUTH
PET HATE: TRAVELLING (DUE TO BROKEN
WINDSCREEN EXPERIENCE WHEN SHE WAS A PUP)

ASHLEY

FAVOURITE TOY: *STICKS OF ANY KIND*
FAVOURITE PASTIME: *CHASING BIRDS*
NAUGHTIEST DEED: *ROLLING IN RABBIT DROPPINGS*
OBSESSION: *BARKING AT HER OTHER RESIDENT GOLDENS*
KNOWN ACCOMPLICES: *FABIAN, VIENNA, DARIUS AND DORIAN*
PET HATE: *BEING CONFINED WHEN EVERYONE ELSE IS RUNNING FREE IN THE VINEYARD*

MILO

KNOWN ACCOMPLICE: NED
FAVOURITE TOY: PLASTIC BOTTLES
NAUGHTIEST DEED: RUNNING AWAY
FAVOURITE PASTIME: RUNNING AWAY
PET HATES: MAGPIES AND WATERBLASTERS
FAVOURITE FOODS: LAMB SHANKS AND GRAPES

PET HATES: WATER AND GUNS
FAVOURITE PASTIMES: GREETING VISITORS
AND USHERING PEOPLE TO THE CELLAR DOOR
FAVOURITE FOODS: A MEATY BONE OR FRESH RABBIT

JEM

ABBEY

PET HATE: *GARY GOING AWAY*
FAVOURITE MOVIE: *101 DALMATIANS*
FAVOURITE TOY: *SQUEAKY RUBBER DUCKY*
KNOWN ACCOMPLICES: *ICE THE JACK RUSSELL PUPPY AND TIGGA THE ADVENTUROUS KITTEN*
OBSESSION: *CHOCOLATE-COATED ROASTED ALMONDS*
NAUGHTIEST DEED: *STEALING GRAPE PICKERS' LUNCHES*

OSCAR

KNOWN ACCOMPLICE: MEG
PET HATE: MEG GETTING THE ATTENTION
FAVOURITE PASTIME: CHASING RABBITS
NAUGHTIEST DEED: SNEAKING INTO
THE CHICKEN COOP AND STEALING EGGS
FAVOURITE TOY: WHATEVER MEG IS PLAYING WITH

FAVOURITE TOY: STONES
FAVOURITE PASTIME: SWIMMING IN THE
AWATERE RIVER AND DIVING FOR STONES
NAUGHTIEST DEED: RUINING THE MOWER
BY LEAVING RIVER STONES ON THE LAWN
PET HATE: WHEN SHE CAN'T CATCH A RABBIT

MEG

PET HATE: HAVING HIS BEARD PULLED
OBSESSION: BEING THE CENTRE OF ATTENTION
KNOWN ACCOMPLICE: FLORRIE THE IRISH TERRIER
FAVOURITE FOOD: HAM, PREFERABLY OFF THE BONE
FAVOURITE PASTIMES: LUXURIATING AND HUMAN MANIPULATION
NAUGHTIEST DEED: STEALING THE VINEYARD WORKERS' LUNCHES OUT OF THE VAN

PET HATE: WINTER
FAVOURITE FOOD: PORRIDGE
FAVOURITE TOY: SHEEP (WELL, WAS BEFORE RETIREMENT)
FAVOURITE PASTIME: WAITING FOR JEREMY TO COME OUT OF THE BAR AT DOG TRIALS
NAUGHTIEST DEED: DECIDING TO HAVE HER FIRST LITTER OF PUPS AT THE RIPE OLD AGE OF 90 DOG YEARS

BID

OWNER: JEREMY RAILTON | HEADING BITCH, 102 (DOG YEARS) | **MT ROSA WINES** CENTRAL OTAGO | 119

PET HATE: WET DAYS
FAVOURITE FOOD: THE PRUNER'S LUNCH
FAVOURITE TOY: CHARISMO, THE BRITISH BLUE CAT
FAVOURITE PASTIME: TESTING SUGAR LEVELS IN GRAPES
KNOWN ACCOMPLICES: CHARISMO AND NEIGHBOUR'S DOGS
NAUGHTIEST DEEDS: CHASING CHOOKS AND SWIMMING IN THE FISH POND

SAINT CLAIR FAMILY ESTATE MARLBOROUGH | LABRADOR, 6 | OWNERS: NEAL AND JUDY IBBOTSON

PET HATE: BEING HUNGRY
FAVOURITE TOY: BEEF BONES
FAVOURITE PASTIME: GETTING PATS
KNOWN ACCOMPLICE: MARTY WATSON
NAUGHTIEST DEED: ESCAPING AND BEING PICKED UP BY
THE MILITARY POLICE ON THE HELIPAD AT WOODBOURNE AIRBASE

SMUDGE

SABI

KNOWN ACCOMPLICE: THE CAT
PET HATES: COLD DAYS AND THE CAT
NAUGHTIEST DEED: EATING A MATTRESS
OBSESSION: EATING VINEYARD WORKERS' LUNCHES
FASTEST MEAL CONSUMED: A WHOLE CAMEMBERT
FAVOURITE PASTIME: PATROLLING THE VINEYARD

FAVOURITE FOODS: CHEESE AND BONES
FAVOURITE TOY: RUBBER GEORGE BUSH HEAD
OBSESSION: CHASING BIRDS AND PASSING HELICOPTERS
FAVOURITE PASTIMES: HANGING OUT WITH SAM THE VINEYARD
MANAGER AND RIDING IN THE UTE WITH THE WIND IN HIS HAIR
PET HATES: STAYING IN THE SHED OR BEING LEFT OUT OF THE ACTION
NAUGHTIEST DEED: CHASING CARS AND HAPLESS TOURISTS ON MOPEDS

JOCK

ATTILA

PET HATE: *OTHER DOGS*
FAVOURITE TOY: *POSSUMS*
FAVOURITE FOOD: *BABY RABBIT SKULLS*
FAVOURITE PASTIMES: *READING, SMOKING AND WATCHING CRICKET*
NAUGHTIEST DEED: *FAILING TO PUT DOWN THE TOILET SEAT AFTER USE*

FAVOURITE MOVIE: LADY AND THE TRAMP
KNOWN ACCOMPLICES: MILLY AND MISSY THE CATS
OBSESSION: BARKING AT HEDGEHOGS IN THE MIDDLE OF THE NIGHT
FAVOURITE PASTIMES: BEING CUDDLED AND NOSING PEOPLE IN THE CROTCH
PET HATE: PEAS – WILL SHOOT THEM OUT HER MOUTH WHEN EATING LEFTOVER FOOD

PIP

OWNERS: THE FINN FAMILY | BEARDED COLLIE X, 10 | **NEUDORF VINEYARDS** NELSON | 125

BEX

PET HATE: *BEING LEFT ALONE*
KNOWN ACCOMPLICE: *MO THE CAT*
FAVOURITE FOOD: *GOURMET LEFTOVERS*
FAVOURITE PASTIME: *WALKING ON THE BEACH*
NAUGHTIEST DEED: *RIPPING OPEN THE RUBBISH BAG*
AND SCATTERING THE CONTENTS THROUGHOUT THE HOUSE
OBSESSION: *CONTROLLING THE PUKEKOS IN THE VINEYARD*

TE MOTU VINEYARD WAIHEKE ISLAND | *JACK RUSSELL TERRIER, 13* | *OWNER: JOHN DUNLEAVY*

PET HATE: THE CAT BEING ALLOWED INTO
BEDROOMS AND LOUNGE WHILE SHE IS NOT
NAUGHTIEST DEED: STEALING THE CAT'S FOOD
FAVOURITE FOOD: ANY FOOD EXCEPT LETTUCE AND TOMATO
FAVOURITE PASTIMES: EATING AND GREETING VISITORS TO THE WINERY

CHLOE

PADDY

FAVOURITE TOY: THE TELEPHONE
OBSESSION: STAFF LUNCH BOXES
FAVOURITE COMIC STRIP: FOOTROT FLATS
NAUGHTIEST DEED: BURYING BONES IN THE VINEYARD
FASTEST MEAL CONSUMED: BOWL OF PRUNES AND FUDGE
KNOWN ACCOMPLICES: NICKY AND MERLOT THE DOG

ODE TO PADDY

by Jane Hunter OBE

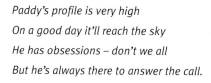

Paddy's profile is very high
On a good day it'll reach the sky
He has obsessions – don't we all
But he's always there to answer the call.

One of his obsessions would have to be food
Staff shouts and lunches put him in the mood
Lunch boxes and what's inside
He'll eat the lot and never hide

Naughtiest deed – where to start
Those loving eyes would melt your heart
Bones in the vineyard – here we go
Just use the front paws – forget the hoe

Pet hates are many – like being alone
Running out of dog biscuits or being left at home
Not being allowed to help Tabitha the cat
Clean up her bowls and sit on her mat

Favourite toys – where would you start
His huge basket full gladdens his heart
A regular one is the telephone
To keep in touch away from home

Fastest meal ever consumed
Would have to be a bowl of prunes
Went right through in half an hour
Man did that take some doggy power

Fudge goes down in 15 seconds
That's what Jane and Belinda reckon
And if the crumbs are on the floor or mat
He'll soon get rid of that

Partners in crime – where would you start
Nicky's the worst – she's got a big heart
Merlot the dog does as he's told
Board member luncheons are a joy to behold

Favourite movie would have to be
The Dog trials on TV
Country Calendar for on-line dating
Would qualify for the highest rating

Favourite books are bedtime stories
Off to sleep with throttled snores
Too short-sighted to read about cats
Just loves Jess from Footrot Flats

Paddy's favourite pastime would have to be
Showing the guests around the winery
Welcoming punters at the cellar door
Lying back on Jane's couch and having a snore.

JANE HUNTER OBE IS ONE OF NEW ZEALAND'S MOST RESPECTED VITICULTURISTS AND HAS CONTRIBUTED TO THE COUNTRY'S IMPACT ON THE INTERNATIONAL WINE COMMUNITY. JANE HAS BEEN OWNER, VITICULTURIST AND MANAGING DIRECTOR OF HUNTER'S WINES SINCE 1987. JANE WAS ALSO NAMED THE INAUGURAL WINNER OF THE WOMEN IN WINE AWARD AT THE GUILDHALL IN LONDON IN 2003.

PET HATE: *BEING LEFT OUT*
FAVOURITE TOY: *TENNIS BALLS*
FAVOURITE TV SHOW: *WIMBLEDON FINALS*
NAUGHTIEST DEED: *EATING ALAN'S GUMBOOTS*
OBSESSIONS: *TENNIS BALLS AND BEING SPIRITUAL*
FASTEST MEAL CONSUMED: *BREAKFAST AND DINNER*
FAVOURITE PASTIME: *FINDING MORE TENNIS BALLS*

TOMMY

TIGGA

FAVOURITE FOOD: POSSUMS
FAVOURITE PASTIMES: SLEEPING AND CHASING SIMBA
NAUGHTIEST DEED: GETTING TO THE CHOOK EGGS FIRST
PET HATE: THE PET RABBIT WHICH CHASES HER ROUND THE YARD

FAVOURITE FOOD: ANYTHING DEAD
PET HATES: THUNDER AND LIGHTNING
FAVOURITE PASTIME: ROUNDING UP THE CHOOKS

SIMBA

CASSIE

PET HATE: RATS
FAVOURITE TOY: ANY STICK
FAVOURITE FOOD: DOG ROLL
KNOWN ACCOMPLICE: JANGO THE CAT
NAUGHTIEST DEED: SWIMMING ACROSS
THE RIVER TO EXPLORE THE OTHER SIDE
FAVOURITE PASTIME: PLAYING WITH JANGO THE CAT

TUPARI WINES MARLBOROUGH | GERMAN SHEPHERD, 3 | OWNER: GLENN THOMAS

OBSESSION: PLAYING WITH UNO THE ROOSTER
FAVOURITE TOYS: UNO THE WINEHOUSE ROOSTER
AND THE FEET OF REBECCA THE ACCOUNTANT
PET HATES: GOOSIE THE GOOSE AND TONY THE PONY
NAUGHTIEST DEED: BEING LESS THAN DISCREET WITH HIS RABBIT
DIGESTION WHEN HE IS SITTING UNDER THE ACCOUNTANT'S DESK
FAVOURITE FOOD: RABBIT HORS D'OEUVRES FROM THE VINEYARD
FAVOURITE PASTIME: SITTING UNDER THE ACCOUNTANT'S DESK

HEMI

BEN

KNOWN ACCOMPLICE: FISH
PET HATE: BIRD SHOOTING IN THE VINEYARD
FAVOURITE PASTIMES: CHASING SHEEP AND SITTING
NEXT TO FISH WITH HIS PAW ON FISH'S HEAD
NAUGHTIEST DEED: SNEAKING INTO THE CHOOK PEN AND EATING THEIR FOOD

PET HATE: BATHS
FAVOURITE FOODS: MEAT, APPLES AND PERSIMMONS
KNOWN ACCOMPLICES: BEN AND TESSA, PAUL'S DAUGHTER
NAUGHTIEST DEED: RUNNING IN FRONT OF A WORKER'S CAR
FAVOURITE PASTIME: BEATING THE UTE AROUND THE VINEYARD

FISH

MOLLY

PET HATE: *BEING TIED UP*
FAVOURITE TOY: *OLD RUGBY BALL*
OBSESSION: *DRAGGING OLD SOCKS*
AND WORK CLOTHES ONTO HER BED
FAVOURITE FOOD: *LEFTOVER ROAST BONES*
FAVOURITE PASTIMES: *SLEEPING AND EATING*
NAUGHTIEST DEED: *SLEEPING WITH THE DOG NEXT DOOR*

FAVOURITE TOY: A BALL OF ANY SORT
KNOWN ACCOMPLICES: GRANDCHILDREN
NICOLE, AIMEE, MASON, BELLA AND BIANCA
PET HATE: WHEN GOLDIE THE CAT EATS ALL OF HIS FOOD
FAVOURITE PASTIME: SWIMMING WITH THE GRANDCHILDREN
FAVOURITE FOOD: ANYTHING – THE VET KEEPS COMPLAINING

SAM

ROSIE

OBSESSION: DIGGING HOLES
FAVOURITE TOY: ABEL THE CAT
PET HATE: THE RUBBISH COLLECTORS
FASTEST MEAL CONSUMED: STOLEN PORK CHOPS
FAVOURITE PASTIME: ROLLING IN DEAD POSSUMS
NAUGHTIEST DEED: ROAMING THE VINEYARD AND ORCHARDS
KNOWN ACCOMPLICES: ANNABEL, JOSEFIEN, RUTGER, RUUD AND DORIEN

FAVOURITE FOODS: SEAFOOD
AND CANNON BONE
FAVOURITE PASTIMES:
CHASING SEAGULLS ON THE
BEACH AND GOING FOR LONG SWIMS
FAVOURITE TOYS: MOWER, TRACTOR AND FORKLIFT
PET HATE: HAVING TO STAY OUTSIDE THE SMOKO ROOM

MUSCAT

TOMI

OBSESSION: ROSS LAWSON
PET HATE: HIGH-ACID CHARDONNAY GRAPES
FASTEST MEAL CONSUMED: 6 LB CHRISTMAS CAKE
FAVOURITE PASTIME: GREETING PEOPLE AT THE CELLAR DOOR
NAUGHTIEST DEED: EATING THE CONTENTS OF THE PANTRY THREE TIMES

TOMI: SHE'S A GRAPE DOG

by Tessa Nicholson

FORGET ALL THAT NEW-FANGLED EQUIPMENT used in vineyards. All you need to tell whether or not it's time to harvest is Tomi the golden labrador.

She's five, extremely rotund, loves licking and is capable of picking a ripe chardonnay grape with just a sniff of her nose. To say nothing of a sauvignon blanc, pinot noir or gewürztraminer.

She even has her own vintage report in a wine magazine, with her nosy sniffs interpreted by her owner Ross Lawson, of Lawson's Dry Hills.

Tomi's penchant for vintage selection was discovered quite early on when, as a pup, she discovered some major advantages of living on a vineyard. Mr Lawson said he didn't realise she was feasting on the fruit until he noticed the grapes were missing from the lower branches of the vines.

"The first time I realised she was eating them was when I discovered there were whole rows for three or four bays without a bloody grape on them. She had been getting underneath the netting and eating them."

Her finely tuned taste developed even further when Mr Lawson was testing individual bunches for their sugar levels, before determining when to harvest.

Squeezing parts of a bunch onto the measuring equipment (a refractometer), he noticed Tomi licking the juice as it fell. Then when he threw the squeezed bunch onto the ground, he noticed Tomi only ever chomped up the bunches that were 22 brix or more (a brix is a measurement of sugar).

Very selective, he thought, until he realised she was also only munching on bunches in the vineyard that had a high sugar level, over 22 brix.

"The sugar level's got to be high and the acid level low before she'll touch them. I know that if I go into a vineyard and she races in and begins chomping, that the grapes are ripe and ready to harvest.

"She can do it on smell alone as well, she does it in the winery. She'll sniff the bunches and ignore, or sniff the bunches and eat. She's got as fat as a porpoise, though."

Tomi could be called a high-class sort of a dog, with chardonnay being her favourite, followed closely by gewürztraminer. And her fame is spreading, with the editor of the magazine Wine NZ dedicating a part of the vintage report especially to Tomi.

And what's more, she doesn't use phrases like 'toasted nuts, yeast, peach and rock melon aromas'. All Tomi does is give an appreciative slurp, which tells most wine drinkers all they need to know.

TESSA NICHOLSON IS A WRITER FOR *THE MARLBOROUGH EXPRESS.*

EDITOR'S NOTE: FOR ALL ASPIRING WINE DOGS OUT THERE – DO NOT EAT GRAPES AS THEY CAN BE TOXIC OR HARMFUL TO YOUR HEALTH (SEE HEALTH WARNING ON PAGE 2). WINE DOGS' MODELS ARE PROFESSIONAL TASTERS AND DO NOT SWALLOW...

PET HATE: BIRDS
FAVOURITE TOY: RUGBY BALL
FAVOURITE FOODS: CHOPS AND SHANK BONES
FAVOURITE PASTIMES: CHASING BIRDS AND SLEEPING
KNOWN ACCOMPLICES: IAN AND THE NEIGHBOUR'S DOG

JESS

PET HATE: CANON FIRE
FAVOURITE PASTIME: WORKING OUT STRATEGIES FOR
GETTING MAXIMUM ATTENTION, THEN BASKING IN IT
KNOWN ACCOMPLICES: JENNY, SAUSIE AND JAMES,
FUDGE THE CAT, NATASHA, THOMAS AND JULIET
NAUGHTIEST DEED: BELIEVING THE MAIN ROAD IS FOR SLEEPING ON

MARS

PET HATES: HEDGEHOGS, BEING LEFT
BEHIND AND ELECTRIC FENCES
FAVOURITE TOY: ANY RETRIEVABLE OBJECT
FAVOURITE PASTIMES: SWIMMING AND CHASING BIRDS
NAUGHTIEST DEED: KILLING THE NEIGHBOUR'S PRIZE CHOOK

MUSTI

COCO

FAVOURITE FOOD: SCRAPS FROM
THE FRENCH BISTRO, MARTINBOROUGH
FAVOURITE PASTIME: GETTING UNDER
JOHN'S FEET WHEN HE'S IN THE WINERY
KNOWN ACCOMPLICES: LIVINGSTONE FROM
NGA WAKA AND MILO FROM ESCARPMENT

PET HATE: BEING IGNORED
OBSESSION: CHASING BIRDS
KNOWN ACCOMPLICE: WILLIE THE DOG
NAUGHTIEST DEED: BARKING WHEN IGNORED
FAVOURITE FOOD: ANYTHING DROPPED AT THE CAFE
FAVOURITE PASTIMES: GREETING TOURISTS AND BEING IN THEIR PHOTOS

JONTY

TETON

PET HATE: FLIES
FAVOURITE TOY: ANY RABBIT
KNOWN ACCOMPLICES: ALL IMAGINARY
FAVOURITE PASTIME: RECYCLING RUBBISH
FAVOURITE FOOD: CENTRAL OTAGO RABBIT
NAUGHTIEST DEED: DESTROYING OWNER'S ENTIRE
CAR UPHOLSTERY AND $1500 WORTH OF SKI GEAR

MOUNT EDWARD WINERY CENTRAL OTAGO | SELECTIVE CROSSBREED 15 | OWNER DUNCAN FORSYTH

FAVOURITE FOOD: RABBITS
KNOWN ACCOMPLICES: HECTOR AND BRIX
PET HATE: OUR NEIGHBOUR ON HIS 4-WHEELER
FAVOURITE PASTIME: CATCHING RABBITS AND HARES
FAVOURITE TOYS: ISOBEL AND MICHAEL'S DAUGHTERS AND HECTOR
NAUGHTIEST DEED: SNEAKING UP ONTO THE SOFA WHEN ALL IS SILENT

ALBI

HECTOR AKA HENK

FAVOURITE TOY: THE BABY, VITA
PET HATE: WALKING ON WET GRASS
KNOWN ACCOMPLICES: BRIX AND ALBI
FAVOURITE PASTIME: RIPPING VITA'S STUFFED
TOYS AND HIDING BEHIND CUSHIONS ON THE SOFA
NAUGHTIEST DEEDS: RIPPING UP TOYS AND EATING THE CARPET

FAVOURITE FOOD: POSTMAN'S THIGH
FAVOURITE PASTIMES: CHASING BIRDS
AND SCARING THE POSTMAN AND RUBBISH MAN
FAVOURITE TOY: ANYTHING SOFT AND FURRY
PET HATES: THE POSTMAN AND RUBBISH MAN
NAUGHTIEST DEED: GOING INTO TOWN AND STEALING
ANYTHING SOFT AND FURRY (TEDDY BEARS, SOCKS, GLOVES)

TED

JAYGAR

OBSESSION: FACEBOOK
FAVOURITE TOY: RUGBY BALL
FAVOURITE FOODS: CHEESEBURGER AND FRIES
PET HATE: WHEN JASON LEAVES THE VINEYARD
NAUGHTIEST DEED: RUNNING THROUGH AN ORGANISED
PHEASANT SHOOT AS HIGH-PAYING CLIENTS TOOK AIM
FAVOURITE PASTIMES: ANNOYING JASON AND CHASING RABBITS

OBSESSION: CLOSE PHYSICAL CONTACT
NAUGHTIEST DEED: DIGGING UP A BABY FERRET AND
CARRYING IT AROUND WHILE CHASING KYLIE O'CONNOR
FAVOURITE FOOD: ANYTHING EXCEPT GREEN VEGETABLES
FAVOURITE TOY: PEOPLE TO PLAY WITH, ESPECIALLY CHILDREN
FAVOURITE PASTIMES: CUDDLING AND HUNTING FOR RABBITS ON THE RIVER BED

FLYNN

*"I named my dog Stay so I can say,
'Come here, Stay... Come here, Stay'."*

———— **STEVEN WRIGHT**

MAX AND MOLLY

MAX'S PET HATE: KENNELS
MAX'S FAVOURITE TOY: BALL

MOLLY'S KNOWN ACCOMPLICES:
MAX AND ARCHIE
MOLLY'S FAVOURITE
FOOD: ANYTHING DIGESTIBLE

KNOWN ACCOMPLICES:
MAX AND MOLLY
FAVOURITE PASTIME:
SWIMMING IN THE WAIRAU RIVER

ARCHIE

MOLLY

PET HATE: *BIG DOGS*
FAVOURITE TOY: *GLOVES*
KNOWN ACCOMPLICE: *JOHNNY*
FAVOURITE PASTIME: *PLAYING*
FAVOURITE FOOD: *WHAT EVERYONE ELSE IS EATING*
NAUGHTIEST DEED: *STEALING A GLOVE OUT OF SOMEONE'S POCKET*

TARA

PET HATE: AUTOMATIC BIRD SCARERS
FAVOURITE PASTIME: ERADICATING RABBITS
FAVOURITE TOY: EMPTY ICE-CREAM CONTAINER, MINUS THE LID
NAUGHTIEST DEED: CHEWING ALL THE EDGES OFF THE COFFEE TABLE
FAVOURITE FOOD: SCOTTY'S OF MARTINBOROUGH FAMOUS BEEF SAUSAGES

FAVOURITE TOY: ROPE PULL TOY
FAVOURITE PASTIME: CHASING TURKEYS
FAVOURITE FOODS: WALNUTS AND GRAPES
NAUGHTIEST DEED: EATING ROTTEN EGGS
KNOWN ACCOMPLICE : GUNNER AND BELLA

ZIN

SHANTI

FAVOURITE FOOD: EGGS
FAVOURITE TOY: RABBIT-FUR MOUSE
FAVOURITE PASTIME: LYING FROG-STYLE
ON THE COOL GROUND ON A SUMMER'S DAY
PET HATES: WATER, TRAVELLING ON THE
FERRY IN STORMY WEATHER, AND THE CAT
NAUGHTIEST DEED: WATCHING TV ON THE COUCH AT THE NEIGHBOUR'S

FAVOURITE TOY: THE CHILDREN
PET HATE: THE WINERY QUAD BIKE
FAVOURITE FOOD: THE CAT'S DINNER
FAVOURITE PASTIMES: LYING ON HER BACK
FOR A RUB OR STANDING BY YOUR SIDE
KNOWN ACCOMPLICE: STORM, THE OTHER WINERY DOG
NAUGHTIEST DEED: CHASING SHEEP INTO THE STREAM

STAR

FIZ

PET HATE: AUTHORITY
FAVOURITE FOOD: RIBEYE BONE
FAVOURITE TOY: STUFFED PARROT
KNOWN ACCOMPLICES: THE BIG DOGS
NAUGHTIEST DEED: NOT COMING
WHEN CALLED BY ROBERT OR LYNDSEY
FAVOURITE PASTIME: CHASING RABBITS

FAVOURITE FOODS: IMPORTED
CHEESE AND STEAK (WITH BONE-IN)
OBSESSION: CREATING A BONE YARD
KNOWN ACCOMPLICES: FIZ AND HARRY
FAVOURITE TOY: KONG IN THE SWIMMING POOL
FAVOURITE PASTIME: RUNNING WITH HIS MATE FIZ
PET HATE: HAVING THE CATS OR FIZ TAKE OVER HIS BED
NAUGHTIEST DEED: EATING 2.5KG OF CHEESE FOR A DINNER PARTY

MAX

MAX

FAVOURITE FOOD: LAMB CHOPS
OBSESSION: CHASING BUNNIES
FAVOURITE TOY: TENNIS BALLS
PET HATE: THE NEIGHBOUR'S CAT
FAVOURITE PASTIME: CHASING BUNNIES
KNOWN ACCOMPLICE: ROCKY THE RABBITER
NAUGHTIEST DEED: EATING A BRAND NEW PAIR OF RUNNING SHOES

OBSESSION: SHOES
KNOWN ACCOMPLICE: MOLLY
FAVOURITE TOY: A SOCCER BALL
FASTEST MEAL CONSUMED: MOTHER'S MILK
FAVOURITE PASTIME: CHASING THE WHEELBARROW

JACKO

KNOWN ACCOMPLICE: JACKO
FAVOURITE PASTIME: CHASING
HIGH-SPEED SOCCER BALLS
OBSESSION: RIDING WITH HER
HEAD OUT THE CAR WINDOW
NAUGHTIEST DEED: STEALING SAUSAGES
PET HATES: LULU THE CAT AND JET PLANES
FAVOURITE TOY: A SQUEAKY BOXING GLOVE

MOLLY

THE MOLLY & JACKO SHOW

by Jo and John Stichbury

WHEN MOLLY BEGAN HER LIFE she had several options but chose to become a winery dog. She had a pedigree as long as your arm, and boy did she know it!

Molly quickly adopted her new home and set about marking the boundaries. Her daily routine was checking the perimeters. Anything that crossed the thin line of Molly's patch was subjected to a vicious attack. Visitors, however, were welcomed with a sniff and a lick, but Molly has a certain aversion to uniforms and makes that very obvious.

In every young lass's life there comes a time when one should take a suitor. Molly, being a long-haired Jack Russell, wished to have her say in the choice. After sometime a young suitor by the name of Boots was found. Boots lived on a rather large ranch and had one or two unmentionable habits. Molly had a weekend with Boots and that was just the beginning. A time later two little boy dogs and three little girl dogs appeared. One was a little round hairy monster and soon became Molly's favourite friend, stayed at the vineyard and was appropriately named Jacko.

Molly taught Jacko all the tricks of the trade but soon developed some of his own. He became a very skilled soccer player and spends hours playing with the ball – pushing it along the ground at high speed and bouncing it on his nose. One skill he did not adopt was road sense and he had a very serious accident. He had friends who carefully nursed him back to health and he is still here with Molly. Jacko has since become very responsible and is forever coming to get help for Molly who gets stuck under containers, concrete floors and wood piles when she has been chasing some unfortunate victim. Kittens and cats around Molly and Jacko quickly develop special climbing skills for their own preservation.

Molly and Jacko are the best of mates and have now expanded their patch covering approximately 42 hectares. They spend hours chasing rabbits, running around in circles barking at the hawks soaring over the vineyard (not realising the hawks are waiting for the dogs to catch the rabbits that are placed on the posts), barking at planes flying over and chasing the ball around.

JACKSON ESTATE WAS FOUNDED IN 1988 BY **JOHN AND JO STICHBURY** WHEN THEY ESTABLISHED
THE HOMESTEAD VINEYARD. THE FIRST WINES WERE RELEASED IN 1991 UNDER THE JACKSON ESTATE LABEL.

BASIL

PET HATE: BEING LEFT IN THE TRUCK
NAUGHTIEST DEED: EATING LUNCHES
FAVOURITE PASTIME: HUNTING RABBITS
KNOWN ACCOMPLICES: ASH AND HARRY
FAVOURITE FOOD: RABBITS AND LUNCHES
OBSESSION: GETTING SCRATCHED BEHIND THE EARS

CARRICK WINES CENTRAL OTAGO | LABRADOR X, 9 | OWNER: GRANT ROLSTON

FAVOURITE TOY: RATA
KNOWN ACCOMPLICE: RATA
PET HATE: NOT GOING TO WORK
FAVOURITE PASTIMES: SUNBATHING AND RABBIT CHASING
NAUGHTIEST DEED: STEALING PINOT FROM THE PICKING BINS
FAVOURITE FOOD: RABBITS WASHED DOWN WITH A BUNCH OF PINOT

MARU

NOUSHKA

PET HATE: FIREWORKS
FAVOURITE FOOD: AVOCADOS
KNOWN ACCOMPLICE: GILMORE THE CAT
FAVOURITE TOY: ANY PIECE OF SHEEPSKIN
FAVOURITE PASTIME: WALKING THE VINES WITH HELMA
NAUGHTIEST DEED: CHASING AND KILLING THE CHOOKS

FAVOURITE FOOD: VENISON
FAVOURITE PASTIME: SLEEPING
FAVOURITE TOY: OLD TENNIS BALL
NAUGHTIEST DEED: POOING ON THE DRIVE
OBSESSION: BEING AT THE WINERY AT 10 O'CLOCK SMOKO

ALBERT

TRIXIE

KNOWN ACCOMPLICE: HARRY
FAVOURITE TOY: BARREL CHOCKS
FAVOURITE FOOD: SEAWEED RICE CRACKERS
NAUGHTIEST DEED: ATTACKING WINE HOSES AS
THEY ARE BEING DRAGGED THROUGH THE WINERY
FAVOURITE PASTIME: CHASING BIRDS AND THE FOUR-WHEELER
PET HATE: SALESMEN ARRIVING UNANNOUNCED AT THE WINERY

KNOWN ACCOMPLICE: TRIXIE
FAVOURITE TOY: SQUEAKY BEAR
PET HATE: HAVING HIS WHISKERS PULLED
FAVOURITE FOOD: SOFT BANANA LOLLIES
FAVOURITE PASTIMES: RIDING IN THE TRACTOR AND CHASING RABBITS
NAUGHTIEST DEED: TEARING BIRD NETTING WHILE CATCHING ENSNARED BIRDS

HARRY

MAX

FAVOURITE FOOD: SAUSAGES
FAVOURITE TOY: SOCCER BALL
PET HATE: THE DISHWASHER DOOR
NAUGHTIEST DEEDS: DIGGING TWO-FEET-DEEP
HOLES AND CHEWING A VISITOR'S SHOE
KNOWN ACCOMPLICES: SAM AND SUCKS, HIS TWO CATS
FAVOURITE PASTIME: RETRIEVING GOLF BALLS AND SOCCER BALLS

FAVOURITE TOY: ANY SOCK
FAVOURITE PASTIME: EATING
PET HATE: BEING LEFT BEHIND
FAVOURITE FOOD: VINEYARD WORKERS' LUNCHES
NAUGHTIEST DEED: STEALING A VISITOR'S WHOLE
CHICKEN DURING TOAST MARTINBOROUGH
KNOWN ACCOMPLICES: MILO FROM ESCARPMENT
AND MAX FROM VAN ZANTEN'S

JAZBO

SOPHIE

FAVOURITE TOY: *BAXTER*
PET HATE: *BEING GROOMED*
KNOWN ACCOMPLICE: *BAXTER*
FAVOURITE FOOD: *ANYTHING BUT LETTUCE*
FAVOURITE PASTIME: *GETTING DIRTY AND WET IN THE POND*
NAUGHTIEST DEED: *GOING OFF TO THE BACK RESERVE AND STAYING AWAY FOR HOURS IN THE PONDS*

PET HATE: *BEING COLD*
FAVOURITE TOY: *SOPHIE*
KNOWN ACCOMPLICE: *SOPHIE*
FAVOURITE FOOD: *DEAD* RABBIT
FAVOURITE PASTIME: *TRYING TO CATCH* RABBITS
NAUGHTIEST DEED: *EATING A FRIEND'S BIRTHDAY CAKE*

BAXTER

SAM

FAVOURITE PASTIMES: DIGGING HOLES
AND BEGGING FOR FOOD AT THE WINERY
FAVOURITE TOY: THE BONE IN HIS BASKET
NAUGHTIEST DEED: GOING WANDERING
PET HATE: BEING TIED UP OUTSIDE BY THE KENNEL
FAVOURITE FOOD: CHICKEN AND VEGETABLE ROLL

FAVOURITE TOY: A TORCH
OBSESSION: SHADOW CHASING
FAVOURITE PASTIME: CHASING SHADOWS
PET HATE: A COUPLE OF FAVOURITE CUSTOMERS
KNOWN ACCOMPLICES: MIA, JOSH AND MADELINE
NAUGHTIEST DEED: EATING HER WAY THROUGH THE LINING ON
THE DOOR OF THE WINERY UTE WHILE CHASING A REFLECTION

FRANKIE

ZAK

OBSESSION: FOOD
KNOWN ACCOMPLICE: OTTO
FAVOURITE PASTIME: SWIMMING
NAUGHTIEST DEED: PINCHING THE WORKERS' LUNCHES

PET HATE: UNFAMILIAR NOISES
OBSESSION: GETTING AS CLOSE TO A LOVED ONE AS POSSIBLE
NAUGHTIEST DEED: RUNNING AWAY WITH HER MUM
FASTEST MEAL CONSUMED: BREAKFAST
KNOWN ACCOMPLICES: OSCAR, LIBBY AND TYSON
FAVOURITE PASTIME: GOING TO THE BEACH

BEAVER

OWNERS: TREVOR AND ROBYN BOLITHO | BOXER, 5 | **WAIMEA ESTATES** NELSON | 183

QUEENIE

FAVOURITE TOY: THE KIDS
FAVOURITE FOOD: HUMAN FOOD
PET HATES: GAS GUNS AND SHOTGUNS
FAVOURITE PASTIME: CHASING RABBITS AND BIRDS

OBSESSION: HUNTING RABBITS
PET HATES: FIREWORKS AND THUNDER
FAVOURITE TOYS: FRISBEE AND SQUEAKY TOY
NAUGHTIEST DEED: BURYING RABBITS IN THE POTATO PATCH
FAVOURITE PASTIME: MEETING AND GREETING VISITORS AT THE CELLAR DOOR
KNOWN ACCOMPLICES: HER CAT SKIPPY AND MICK, THE NEIGHBOUR'S JACK RUSSELL

CASSIE

BAXTER

PET HATE: RIDE-ON LAWN MOWERS
KNOWN ACCOMPLICES: EMILY AND SOPHIE
FAVOURITE TOY: EMPTY ICE-CREAM CONTAINER
NAUGHTIEST DEED: CHEWING HIS BRAND NEW BED
FAVOURITE PASTIME: MOOCHING AROUND THE CELLAR DOOR,
SUPERVISING SMOKO AND LUNCH BREAKS

ON THE PERILS
OF PHOTOGRAPHING WINE DOGS

by Bob Campbell

"GET BACK HERE YA MONGREL", yelled Mike, somehow managing to inject a little affection into the command. Shorty, his wiry Jack Russell of uncertain age, shot through the vines in hot pursuit of a rabbit. "The little bastard, once he gets the scent of an animal, years of training go out the window", complained Mike as we picked our way toward the top of the vineyard.

When we reached the crest of the hill Shorty was furiously digging his way into a rabbit burrow. It was a crisp summer's day in Central Otago. We gazed across an arid landscape of brown hills relieved here and there by patchworks of vineyard, their new green leaves offering a welcome contrast to dusty soil. In the distance Lake Dunstan lay like a sparkling blue ribbon at the base of dark hills still capped with the last of the winter snow.

"If the useless bugger put as much energy into running as she did into sinking her teeth into photographers we'd have won the trophy last year", drawled Mike, needing little encouragement to relate the whole dramatic saga.

Mike explained that the highlight of the annual Wanaka Agricultural and Pastoral Show is the Jack Russell race. Wanaka is a wine-growing district in Central Otago, some distance from Mike's own vineyard in the even more famous wine district of Bannockburn.

"It's a pretty competitive event", he explained. "Most of the High Country sheep farmers and many of Wanaka's grape growers own Jack Russells. There's an epidemic of rabbits in the district so it's good to have a dog that'll give them a bit of a hurry-up", he said, glancing in the direction of Shorty, who was now tunnelling around a metre underground.

"They don't like outsiders competing against local dogs, so I had to elbow my way onto the starting line where 60–70 owners restrained their restless dogs. I can tell you that I got quite a few dirty looks.

"A bloke on a horse came onto the race track towing a dead rabbit on a rope behind him. He dragged the rabbit a few metres in front of the drooling, barking Jack Russells before turning and dragging the rabbit just half a metre away from the dogs. They went absolutely berserk.

"As the horseman was working the dogs into a lather, a photographer from the Otago Daily Times calmly walked into the middle of the track, lay down and trained his telephoto lens on the pack. An official, spotting the potential for trouble, made an announcement over the loudspeaker, asking the photographer to get clear of the track. The horseman spun around in his saddle and shouted at the photographer to 'bugger off'. Ignoring both requests,s the photographer waved his hand in an 'I'll be all right' motion and began fiddling with his camera.

"A starter gun fired and the horseman charged down the track dragging the bouncing carcass behind him, with a pack of blood-crazed dogs in hot pursuit. As he drew alongside the photographer the rabbit swung wide on its lead which wrapped around the photographer's neck. The man on the horse wisely let go the rope to avoid strangling the photographer.

"There was a gasp from the crowd as they witnessed the photographer's predicament. There he was, lying on the ground, with a dead rabbit on his chest as 60 to 70 red-eyed, saliva-specked, howling dogs leapt onto him. It was total chaos. The photographer's struggling body was completely hidden by a sea of Jack Russell backsides as the business ends tried to do a bit of damage.

"The bloke on the horse did his best to rescue the situation. Leaping from the saddle, he grabbed the rope, re-mounted the horse and continued his race toward the finish line. Only about half the dogs followed him. The rest preferred a live photographer to a dead rabbit. Officials ran onto the track and began tearing dogs from the writhing body. Shorty was the last to let go.

"An ambulance was called and they carted the photographer away. It was later reported that he had 163 bites to his body. They patched him up but I bet he now gets a bit twitchy when he comes across a Jack Russell."

By now Shorty had caught the rabbit and consumed about half of it. I glanced at her with a new respect and saw that she was staring at me with a fixed and slightly deranged gaze. Very slowly I eased my camera into my backpack. We both relaxed.

BOB CAMPBELL MW IS A MASTER OF WINE AND NEW ZEALAND'S BEST-KNOWN WINE WRITER, JUDGE AND EDUCATOR. HE'S CURRENTLY OWNED BY A LARGE (8.5 KG) CAT BUT PLANS TO ADOPT A DOG (SMALL, BUT NOT A JACK RUSSELL) WHEN THE TIME IS RIGHT.

KEVIN JUDD

PHOTOGRAPHER *MARLBOROUGH, NZ*

KEVIN JUDD IS CHIEF WINEMAKER AT CLOUDY BAY VINEYARDS IN MARLBOROUGH, NEW ZEALAND, WHERE HE HAS BEEN RESPONSIBLE FOR THE DEVELOPMENT OF THE COMPANY'S RANGE OF WINES SINCE ITS INCEPTION IN 1985, INCLUDING THE INTERNATIONALLY RENOWNED CLOUDY BAY SAUVIGNON BLANC.

OVER THE LAST TWO DECADES, KEVIN HAS ALSO BECOME RECOGNISED AS ONE OF THE WORLD'S GREAT WINE PHOTOGRAPHERS. HIS VIBRANT VINEYARD LANDSCAPES OF NEW ZEALAND AND NUMEROUS OTHER COUNTRIES HAVE APPEARED IN MANY PUBLICATIONS AND EXHIBITIONS AROUND THE WORLD. HIS FIRST BOOK, *THE COLOUR OF WINE*, WAS PUBLISHED IN 1999 TO MUCH CRITICAL ACCLAIM, AND HE HAS SUBSEQUENTLY ILLUSTRATED A NUMBER OF OTHER BOOKS, INCLUDING *THE GREAT WINES OF NEW ZEALAND* AND *TASTE OF THE EARTH* BY KEITH STEWART.

KEVIN ALSO SHOT ALL THE KIWI DOGS FOR *WINE DOGS DELUXE EDITION*.

IN CONJUNCTION WITH CRAIG POTTON PUBLISHING, KEVIN IS CURRENTLY FINALISING CONTENT FOR HIS SECOND BOOK, *THE LANDSCAPE OF NEW ZEALAND WINE*, DUE FOR RELEASE IN 2009, WHICH PROMISES TO PROVIDE A SPECTACULAR JOURNEY THROUGH THE STUNNING SCENERY OF NEW ZEALAND'S VITICULTURAL REGIONS — ALL THE WAY FROM THE BAY OF ISLANDS TO BENDIGO.

KEVIN, KIMBERLEY AND THEIR TWO SONS KOHEN AND ALEX LIVE IN MARLBOROUGH SURROUNDED BY VINEYARDS IN THE PICTURESQUE OMAKA VALLEY.

AFTER HE PHOTOGRAPHED FOR *WINE DOGS NEW ZEALAND* WE CAN NOW ARGUE A CASE FOR KEVIN BEING CONSIDERED AS ONE OF THE WORLD'S GREAT DOG PHOTOGRAPHERS, AND HE HAS PROMISED NOT TO TAKE LEGAL ACTION FOR THE MAULED FINGERS OBTAINED DURING THE PRODUCTION OF THIS BOOK. MORE OF KEVIN'S OUTSTANDING PHOTOGRAPHS CAN BE VIEWED AT WWW.KEVINJUDD.CO.NZ

Kevin and Dixie

PHOTOGRAPH © JIM TANNOCK PHOTOGRAPHY 2008

FAVOURITE FOOD: ANYTHING OFF THE BARBIE

FAVOURITE PASTIMES: SHOOTING DOGS AND DRINKING CHARDONNAY

NAUGHTIEST DEED: WAGGING WORK WHEN THE LIGHT IS RIGHT

OBSESSIONS: WINE AND BEING THERE WHEN THE LIGHT IS RIGHT

KNOWN ACCOMPLICES: DIXIE, ROVER AND RHIANNON

PET HATES: PERSONALISED PLATES AND POSH ACCENTS

FAVOURITE TOY: PHOTOSHOP

SUSAN ELLIOTT

AUTHOR / PUBLISHER *SYDNEY, NSW*

SUSAN IS A MULTI-SKILLED ARTIST WITH A BACKGROUND IN FINE ART, ILLUSTRATION AND PRINTMAKING. AFTER COMPLETING TWO YEARS OF A PSYCHOLOGY DEGREE, SUE CHANGED TO A CAREER IN ART. SHE GRADUATED FROM THE CITY ART INSTITUTE IN 1986, MAJORING IN DRAWING, PRINTMAKING AND PAINTING.

AFTER TWO YEARS LIVING ABROAD, SUE RETURNED TO AUSTRALIA AND EXHIBITED HER GRAPHIC ART AND SCREENPRINTS EXTENSIVELY AROUND SYDNEY, WHILE ALSO WORKING IN A NUMBER OF SMALL DESIGN STUDIOS. SHE HAS DEVELOPED INTO AN AWARD-WINNING GRAPHIC DESIGNER WITH OVER 20 YEARS OF EXPERIENCE IN THE INDUSTRY.

SUE JOINED McGILL DESIGN GROUP IN 1999 AS CO-OWNER AND CREATIVE DIRECTOR. SHE IS ALSO CO-FOUNDER AND PRINCIPAL OF THE GIANT DOG PUBLISHING HOUSE, WHICH IS RESPONSIBLE FOR PRODUCING A NUMBER OF BEST-SELLING BOOKS, INCLUDING THE WINE DOGS AND FOOTY DOGS TITLES.

Stella and Sue

PHOTOGRAPH © CRAIG McGILL 2008

FAVOURITE FOOD: NOODLES
OBSESSIONS: BATH SALTS AND CRYPTIC CROSSWORDS
FAVOURITE PASTIME: WATCHING MOVIES WITH STELLA
NAUGHTIEST DEED: TEASING HUSKIES
KNOWN ACCOMPLICE: CASPER THE GHOST KNIFE FISH
PET HATES: WHISTLING AND RAISIN TOAST WITH PEEL

SUE'S KNOWLEDGE OF DOGS IS UNPARALLELED, AND IN THE PAST SHE HAS ALSO FOUND TIME TO BE A SUCCESSFUL SIBERIAN HUSKY BREEDER. SHE IS CONSIDERED AMONGST THE PACK TO BE A GREAT OWNER. SUE IS A LOVER OF ALL WHITE WINE AND USUALLY REACHES FOR HER FAVOURITE RIESLING WHEN FEELING A LITTLE HUSKY.

GIANT DOG PUBLISHING

GIANT DOG IS A NICHE INDEPENDENT PUBLISHING HOUSE SPECIALISING IN PRODUCING BENCHMARK QUALITY DESIGN AND ART BOOKS. RECENT PUBLICATIONS INCLUDE *WINE DOGS ITALY*, *WINE DOGS AUSTRALIA*, *WINE DOGS NEW ZEALAND*, *WINE DOGS DELUXE EDITION*, *FOOTY DOGS* AND *WINE DOGS: USA EDITION*. www.giantdog.com.au

CRAIG McGILL

AUTHOR / PUBLISHER *SYDNEY, NSW*

ORIGINALLY FROM SHEPPARTON, VICTORIA, CRAIG IS A SELF-TAUGHT DESIGNER AND ILLUSTRATOR WHO STARTED HIS OWN DESIGN BUSINESS IN MELBOURNE AT 18 YEARS OF AGE. DURING THAT TIME HE WAS APPOINTED AS A DESIGN CONSULTANT TO THE RESERVE BANK OF AUSTRALIA.

HIS DESIGNS AND ILLUSTRATIONS HAVE GRACED BANKNOTES THROUGHOUT THE WORLD, INCLUDING THE AUSTRALIAN BICENTENARY TEN-DOLLAR NOTE. HIS WORK APPEARS ON THE ORIGINAL AUSTRALIAN $100 NOTE, PAPUA NEW GUINEA KINA, COOK ISLAND DOLLARS AND ENGLISH POUND TRAVELLER'S CHEQUES. CRAIG WAS ALSO INVOLVED IN THE DESIGN AND ILLUSTRATION OF MANY COUNTRIES' SECURITY DOCUMENTS SUCH AS PASSPORTS, BONDS AND TRAVELLER'S CHEQUES.

AT THE AGE OF 23 HE DESIGNED THE ENTIRE SERIES OF THE COOK ISLAND BANKNOTES AND IT IS BELIEVED THAT HE WAS THE WORLD'S YOUNGEST DESIGNER TO DESIGN A COUNTRY'S COMPLETE CURRENCY. IN 1991, CRAIG MOVED TO SYDNEY WHERE HIS ILLUSTRATIONS WERE REGULARLY COMMISSIONED BY AGENCIES AND DESIGNERS BOTH IN AUSTRALIA AND AROUND THE WORLD.

Craig and Tarka

PHOTOGRAPH © SUSAN ELLIOTT 2008

DATE OF BIRTH: DEAD IN DOG YEARS

FAVOURITE FOOD: ROAST DUCK AND PINOT NOIR

FAVOURITE PASTIMES: VENTRILOQUISM AND BEING A BIG KID

NAUGHTIEST DEED: CHASING HUSKIES WHILE STARK NAKED

OBSESSIONS: BEER, WINE AND COLLECTING USELESS THINGS

KNOWN ACCOMPLICES: THE VOICES IN MY HEAD

PET HATE: UNORIGINAL IDEAS

HE IS NOW WIDELY KNOWN AS AUSTRALIA'S ONLY FREELANCE CURRENCY DESIGNER. CRAIG HAS ALSO DESIGNED AND ILLUSTRATED FIVE STAMPS FOR AUSTRALIA POST.

CRAIG HAS BEEN CREATIVE DIRECTOR OF HIS OWN AGENCY, McGILL DESIGN GROUP, FOR OVER TWENTY-THREE YEARS.

HAVING GROWN UP WITH A SUCCESSION OF BEAGLES, CRAIG IS NOW OWNED BY TWO SIBERIAN HUSKIES. www.realnasty.com.au

McGILL DESIGN GROUP

McGILL DESIGN GROUP WAS FORMED IN 1981 AND SPECIALISES IN PROVIDING A WIDE RANGE OF QUALITY GRAPHIC DESIGN SERVICES. THE STUDIO HAS PRODUCED NUMEROUS FINE WINE LABELS AND PACKAGING AS WELL AS CORPORATE IDENTITIES, ADVERTISING, PUBLICATIONS AND TELEVISION COMMERCIALS. www.mcgilldesigngroup.com

WINERY and VINEYARD LISTINGS

AUCKLAND & WAIHEKE ISLAND

Babich Wines PAGE 67
9 Babich Road,
Henderson Valley,
Waitakere, Auckland 0614
Ph: (09) 833 7859
www.babichwines.co.nz

Cable Bay Vineyards PAGE 123
12 Nick Johnstone Drive,
Oneroa, Waiheke Island
Ph: (09) 372 5889
www.cablebayvineyards.co.nz

Coopers Creek Vineyard
PAGES 30, 31
601 State Highway 16,
Huapai, Auckland 0841
Ph: (09) 412 8560
www.cooperscreek.co.nz

Goldwater Estate PAGE 162
18 Causeway Road,
Putiki Bay, Waiheke Island
Ph: (09) 372 7493
www.goldwaterwine.com

Matua Valley Wines PAGE 78
Waikoukou Valley Road,
Waimauku, Auckland
Ph: (09) 411 8301
www.matua.co.nz

Mudbrick Vineyard
PAGES 82, 83
126 Church Bay Road,
Oneroa, Waiheke Island
Ph: (09) 372 9050
www.mudbrick.co.nz

Stonyridge Vineyard PAGE 54
80 Onetangi Road,
Waiheke Island
Ph: (09) 372 8766
www.stonyridge.com

Te Motu Vineyard PAGE 126
76 Onetangi Road,
Waiheke Island
Ph: (09) 372 6884
www.temotu.co.nz

Te Whau Vineyard PAGE 141
218 Te Whau Drive,
Oneroa, Waiheke Island
Ph: (09) 372 7191
www.tewhau.com

GISBORNE

Brunton Road Wines PAGE 102
*189 Riverpoint Road,
RD1 Gisborne
Ph: (06) 967 6140
www.bruntonroad.co.nz*

Kirkpatrick Estate Winery
PAGES 174, 175
*569 Wharekopae Road,
RD2 Gisborne
Ph: (06) 862 7722
www.kew.co.nz*

Stone Bridge Vineyard
PAGES 98, 99
*70 Newstead Lane,
RD1 Gisborne
Ph: (06) 867 7140
www.stonebridgewine.com*

Tiritiri Vineyard PAGES 132, 133
*1646 Waimata Valley
Road, Gisborne
Ph: (06) 867 0372
www.tiritiriestate.com*

TW Wines PAGES 136–138
*853 Back Ormond Road,
RD1 Gisborne
Ph: (06) 868 6499
www.twwines.co.nz*

Waimata Wines PAGE 55
*Upper Stout Street, Gisborne
Ph: 027 201 4774
www.waimata.ac.nz*

HAWKES BAY

Askerne PAGES 64, 65
*267 Te Mata Mangateretere
Road, Havelock North,
Hawkes Bay
Ph: (06) 877 2089
www.askerne.co.nz*

Black Barn Vineyard PAGE 68
*Black Barn Road RD12,
Havelock North, Hawkes Bay
Ph: (06) 877 7985
www.blackbarn.com*

Brookfields Vineyards
PAGE 103
*376 Brookfields Road,
Meeanee, Napier,
Hawkes Bay
Ph: (06) 834 4615
www.brookfieldsvineyards.co.nz*

C J Pask Winery PAGE 173
*1133 Omahu Road, Hastings,
Hawkes Bay
Ph: (06) 879 7906
www.cjpaskwinery.co.nz*

Clearview Estate PAGE 172
*194 Clifton Road, Te Awanga,
RD2 Hastings, Hawkes Bay
Ph: (06) 875 0150
www.clearviewestate.co.nz*

Craggy Range Vineyards
PAGE 111
*253 Waimarama Road,
Havelock North, Hawkes Bay
Ph: (06) 873 7126
www.craggyrange.com*

**Crossroads Winery (Ager
Sectus Wine Estates)**
PAGE 70
*1747 Korokipo Road,
Napier, Hawkes Bay
Ph: (06) 879 9737
www.crossroadswinery.co.nz*

Esk Valley Estate PAGES 38, 39
*Main Road, Bay View,
Napier, Hawkes Bay
Ph: (06) 872 7432
www.eskvalley.co.nz*

HAWKES BAY *continued*

Hatton Estate PAGE 163
124 Gimblett Road, RD5
Hastings, Hawkes Bay
Ph: (06) 870 4777
www.hattonestate.com

Kemblefield Estate
PAGE 161
Kemblefield Terrace RD1,
Hastings, Hawkes Bay
Ph: (06) 874 9649
www.kemblefield.co.nz

Kim Crawford Wines
PAGES 72, 73
Clifton Road, Te Awanga,
RD2 Hastings, Hawkes Bay
Ph: (06) 875 0553
www.kimcrawford
wines.co.nz

Lime Rock Wines PAGE 77
601 Tikokino Road,
Waipawa, Hawkes Bay
Ph: (06) 857 8247
www.limerock.co.nz

Matariki Wines PAGE 155
52 Kirkwood Road, RD5,
Hastings, Hawkes Bay 4175
Ph: (06) 879 6226
www.matarikiwines.co.nz

Mission Estate Winery
PAGE 42
198 Church Road, Taradale,
Napier, Hawkes Bay
Ph: (06) 845 9350
www.missionestate.co.nz

Ngatarawa Wines PAGE 180
305 Ngatarawa Road, RD5,
Hastings, Hawkes Bay
Ph: (06) 879 7603
www.ngatarawa.co.nz

Sacred Hill Wines
PAGES 48, 49
1033 Dartmoor Road,
Puketapu, Napier,
Hawkes Bay
Ph: (06) 844 0138
www.sacredhill.com

Sileni Estates PAGE 56
2016 Maraekakaho Rd, RD1,
Hastings, Hawkes Bay
Ph: (06) 879 8768
www.sileni.co.nz

Stonecroft PAGE 131
RD5 Mere Rd, Hastings,
Hawkes Bay
Ph: (06) 879 9610
www.stonecroft.co.nz

Te Awa PAGES 22, 23
2375 State Highway 50
RD5, Hastings, Hawkes Bay
Ph: (06) 879 7602
www.teawa.com

Villa Maria Estate
PAGES 28, 29
See listing under
Marlborough

Zepelin Wines PAGE 139
275 Te Mata Road, RD12,
Havelock North, Hawkes Bay
Ph: (06) 877 1477
www.zepelin.co.nz

WAIRARAPA

Ata Rangi Vineyard PAGE 24
Puruatanga Road,
Martinborough, Wairarapa
Ph: (06) 306 9570
www.atarangi.co.nz

Benfield & Delamare PAGE 66
35 New York Street,
Martinborough, Wairarapa
Ph: (06) 306 9926
www.benfieldanddelamare.co.nz

Cabbage Tree Vineyard, The
PAGES 108, 109
52 Kitchener Street,
Martinborough, Wairarapa
Ph: (06) 306 8178
www.thecabbagetree
 vineyard.co.nz

Canadoro Wines PAGES 112, 113
125 New York Street,
Martinborough, Wairarapa
Ph: (06) 306 8801

Claddagh Vineyard PAGE 177
Puruatanga Road,
Martinborough, Wairarapa
Ph: (06) 306 9264
www.claddagh.co.nz

Coney Wines PAGE 71
Dry River Road, RD1, 5954
Martinborough, Wairarapa
Ph: (06) 306 8345
www.coneywines.co.nz

Escarpment Vineyard PAGE 114
Te Muna Road,
Martinborough, Wairarapa
Ph: (06) 306 8305
www.escarpment.co.nz

Gladstone Vineyard
PAGES 178, 179
Gladstone Road, RD2,
Carterton, Wairarapa
Ph: (06) 379 8563
www.gladstone.co.nz

Julicher Estate PAGE 160
301 Te Muna Road,
Martinborough, Wairarapa
Ph: (06) 306 8575
www.julicher.co.nz

Linacre Lane Wines PAGE 74
Puruatanga Road,
Martinborough, Wairarapa
Ph: (06) 306 9026

Loopline Vineyard PAGE 145
42 Loop Line, Opaki, RD1,
Masterton, Wairarapa
Ph: (06) 377 3353
www.loopline.co.nz

Martinborough Vineyards
PAGE 81
Princess Street,
Martinborough, Wairarapa
Ph: (06) 306 9955
www.martinborough-vineyard.com

Martinus Estate PAGE 176
117 Todds Road, RD4,
Martinborough, Wairarapa
Ph: (06) 306 9449
www.martinus.co.nz

Mebus Estate PAGES 151, 152
Dakins Road, RD7,
Masterton, Wairarapa
Ph: (06) 377 3696
www.mebusestate.co.nz

Murdoch James PAGES 94, 95
Dry River Road,
Martinborough, Wairarapa
Ph: (06) 306 9165
www.murdochjames.co.nz

Nga Waka Vineyard PAGE 80
Kitchener Street,
Martinborough, Wairarapa
Ph: (06) 306 9832
www.ngawaka.co.nz

Palliser Estate PAGES 146, 147
Kitchener Street,
Martinborough, Wairarapa
Ph: (06) 306 9019
www.palliser.co.nz

Pond Paddock Vineyard
PAGE 184
248 Te Muna Road,
Martinborough, Wairarapa
Ph: (06) 306 8114
www.pondpaddock.co.nz

Porters Pinot PAGE 148
47 Kitchener Street,
Martinborough, Wairarapa
Ph: (06) 306 9013
www.porterspinot.co.nz

**Stratford Wines of
Martinborough** PAGE 153
115 New York Street,
Martinborough, Wairarapa
Ph: (06) 306 9257
www.stratford.co.nz

Te Kairanga PAGE 101
89 Martins Road,
Martinborough,
Wairarapa 5784
Ph: (06) 306 9122
www.tekairanga.co.nz

MARLBOROUGH

Allan Scott Wines PAGES 1, 104
Jacksons Road, RD3,
Blenheim, Marlborough
Ph: (03) 572 9054

Cloudy Bay Vineyards
PAGES 6, 11–16
Jacksons Road,
Blenheim, Marlborough
Ph: (03) 520 9140
www.cloudybay.co.nz

Dog Point Vineyard
PAGES 20, 21
Dog Point Road, RD2,
Blenheim, Marlborough
Ph: (03) 572 8294
www.dogpoint.co.nz

Domaine Georges Michel
PAGE 96
56 Vintage Lane, RD3
Blenheim, Marlborough
Ph: (03) 572 7230
www.georgesmichel.co.nz

Forrest Estate Winery
PAGE 59
19 Blicks Road,
Renwick, Marlborough
Ph: (03) 572 9084
www.forrest.co.nz

Fromm Winery PAGES 46, 47
Godfrey Road, RD2, Blenheim,
Marlborough 7272
Ph: (03) 572 9355
www.frommwinery.co.nz

Grove Mill PAGE 18
Waihopai Valley Road,
Renwick, Marlborough
Ph: (03) 572 8200
www.grovemill.co.nz

Herzog Winery PAGE 122
81 Jeffries Road,
Blenheim, Marlborough
Ph: (03) 572 8770
www.herzog.co.nz

Highfield PAGE 19
Brookby Road, RD2,
Blenheim, Marlborough
Ph: (03) 572 9244
www.highfield.co.nz

Hunter's Wines PAGE 128
Rapaura Road, Blenheim,
Marlborough
Ph: (03) 572 8489
www.hunters.co.nz

Jackson Estate PAGE 142
PO Box 102, Renwick,
Marlborough
Ph: (03) 579 5523
www.jacksonestate.co.nz

Lawson's Dry Hills PAGE 142
Alabama Road, Blenheim,
Marlborough
Ph: (03) 578 7674
www.lawsonsdryhills.co.nz

Montana Wines PAGE 117
RD4 Riverlands (State Highway
One), Blenheim, Marlborough
Ph: (03) 578 2099
www.montanawines.co.nz

Mount Riley Wines PAGE 93
10 Malthouse Road, Riverlands,
RD4, Blenheim, Marlborough
Ph: (03) 577 9900
www.mountriley.co.nz

Nautilus Estate PAGE 84
12 Rapaura Road, Renwick,
Marlborough
Ph: (03) 572 9364
www.nautilusestate.com

No. 1 Family Estate PAGE 97
169 Rapaura Road, RD3,
Blenheim, Marlborough
Ph: (03) 572 9876
www.no1familyestate.co.nz

Richardson Wines PAGE 79
Ph: +64 21 584 284
www.richardsonwines.co.nz

Riverby Estate PAGES 44, 45
RD3 Jacksons Road,
Blenheim, Marlborough
Ph: (03) 578 9931
www.riverbyestate.com

Saint Clair Family Estate
PAGE 120
Corner Rapaura and
Selmes Roads, Marlborough
Ph: (03) 570 5280
www.saintclair.co.nz

Seresin Estate PAGE 43
85 Bedford Road, RD1,
Renwick, Marlborough
Ph: (03) 572 9408
www.seresin.co.nz

Spy Valley Wines PAGE 57
37 Lake Timara Road, RD6,
Blenheim, Marlborough
Ph: (03) 572 9840
www.spyvalleywine.co.nz

Staete Landt Vineyard
PAGE 140
275 Rapaura Rd,
Blenheim, Marlborough
Ph: (03) 572 9886
www.staetelandt.co.nz

Stoneleigh Vineyards
PAGE 121
299 Jacksons Road,
Blenheim, Marlborough
Ph: (03) 572 8677
www.stoneleigh.co.nz

Te Whare Ra Wines PAGE 186
56 Anglesea Street,
Renwick, Marlborough
Ph: (03) 572 8581
www.tewharera.co.nz

The Ned PAGE 69
Guernsey Road, Waihopai
Valley, Marlborough
Ph: 027 66 99 143
www.thened.co.nz

Tupari Wines PAGE 134
660 Dillons Point Road, RD3,
Blenheim, Marlborough
Ph: (03) 578 0913
www.tupari.co.nz

Vavasour Wines PAGE 58
1549 Redwood Pass Road, RD4,
Blenheim, Marlborough
Ph: (03) 575 7481
www.vavasour.com

Villa Maria Estate
PAGES COVER, 25–29
Marlborough Cellar Door:
Corner Payntors and New
Renwick Roads, Blenheim,
Marlborough
Ph: (03) 520 8470

Head Office and
Auckland Cellar Door:
118 Montgomerie Road,
Mangere, Auckland
Ph: (09) 255 0660
www.villamaria.co.nz

Wither Hills Vineyards
PAGE 63
211 New Renwick Road,
RD2, Blenheim, Marlborough
Ph: (03) 520 8270
www.witherhills.co.nz

Wairau River Wines PAGE 157
264 Rapaura Road, RD3,
Blenheim, Marlborough
Ph: (03) 572 7950
www.wairauriverwines.com

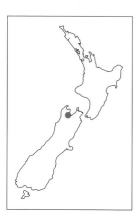

NELSON

Brightwater Vineyard
PAGE 116
546 Main Road, Hope, Nelson
Ph: (03) 544 1066
www.brightwaterwine.co.nz

Neudorf Vineyards PAGE 125
Neudorf Road,
Upper Moutere, Nelson
Ph: (03) 543 2643
www.neudorf.co.nz

Waimea Estates PAGES 110, 183
Appleby Highway,
Hope, Nelson
Ph: (03) 544 6385
www.waimeaestates.co.nz

CANTERBURY

Camshorn Vineyard PAGE 171
460 Glasnevin Road RD2,
Amberley, North Canterbury
Ph: (03) 314 7396
www.pernod-ricard-nz.com

Fiddler's Green Wines PAGE 115
Georges Road, Waipara,
North Canterbury
Ph: (03) 314 6979
www.fiddlersgreen.co.nz

Mount Cass Wines PAGE 185
133 Mount Cass Road, Waipara,
North Canterbury
Ph: (03) 314 6834
www.mountcasswines.com

Mountford Vineyard
PAGES 32, 35
434 Omihi Road, Waipara,
North Canterbury
Ph: (03) 314 6819

Pegasus Bay PAGES 36, 37
Stockgrove Road, Waipara
RD2 Amberley 7482
North Canterbury
Ph: (03) 314 6869
www.pegasusbay.com

Pyramid Valley Vineyards
PAGES 86, 87
548 Pyramid Valley Road,
RD Waikari 7491,
North Canterbury
Ph: (03) 314 2006
www.pyramidvalley.co.nz

Sherwood Estate PAGE 17
PO Box 100, Church Road,
Waipara, 8270
North Canterbury
Ph: (03) 314 6962
www.sherwood.co.nz

Torlesse Wines PAGE 127
Loffhagen Drive, Waipara,
8270 North Canterbury
Ph: (03) 314 6929
www.torlesse.co.nz

Waipara Springs Winery
PAGE 149
409 Omihi Road, Waipara,
North Canterbury
Ph: (03) 314 6777
www.waiparasprings.co.nz

OTAGO

Akarua PAGES 158, 159
Rapid Number 210,
Cairnmuir Road, Bannockburn,
Central Otago 9384
Ph: (03) 445 0897
www.akarua.com

Amisfield PAGES 4, 88
10 Lake Hayes Road, RD1
Queenstown, Central Otago
Ph: (03) 442 0556
www.amisfield.co.nz

Bald Hills Vineyard
PAGES 50, 51
Cornish Point Road,
Bannockburn, Central Otago
Ph: (03) 445 3161
www.baldhills.co.nz

Carrick Wines PAGE 170
Bannockburn, RD2,
Cromwell, Central Otago
Ph: (03) 445 3480

**Central Otago Wine
Company** PAGE 124
102 Gair Avenue, Cromwell,
Central Otago
Ph: (03) 445 3100
www.cowine.co.nz

Cornish Point PAGE 40
319 Felton Road, RD2
Bannockburn,
Central Otago
Ph: (03) 445 0885
www.cornishpoint.co.nz

De Vine Wines PAGE 53
PO Box 244, Arrowtown,
Central Otago
Ph: 64 21 274 3369
www.devinewines.co.nz

Felton Road PAGE 41
319 Felton Road, RD2
Bannockburn, 9384
Central Otago
Ph: (03) 445 0885
www.feltonroad.com

Gibbston Valley Wines
PAGE 52
Gibbston RD1, State Highway 6,
Queenstown, Central Otago
Ph: (03) 442 6910
www.gvwines.co.nz

Leaning Rock Vineyard
PAGE 75
188 Hillview Road, RD1
Alexandra, Central Otago
Ph: (03) 448 9169
www.leaningrock.co.nz

Love Family Vineyard PAGE 76
140 Hillview Road,
Alexandra, Central Otago
Ph: (03) 448 7172
www.jameslovewine.com

Mount Edward Winery
PAGE 150
34 Coalpit Road, RD1
Queenstown, Central Otago
Ph: (03) 442 6113
www.mountedward.co.nz

Mt Difficulty PAGE 181
73 Felton Road, RD2
Cromwell, Central Otago
Ph: (03) 445 3445
www.mtdifficulty.co.nz

Mt Rosa Wines PAGES 118, 119
109 Gibbston Back Road, RD1
Queenstown, Central Otago
Ph: (03) 441 2493
www.mtrosa.co.nz

Peregrine Wines PAGE 85
Kawarau Gorge Road, RD1
Queenstown, Central Otago
Ph: (03) 442 4000
www.peregrinewines.co.nz

**Rippon Vineyard
and Winery** PAGES 90–92
246 Mt Aspiring Road,
Wanaka, Central Otago
Ph: (03) 443 8084
www.rippon.co.nz

Sublime Vineyards Otago
PAGE 100
Rapid 511 Grants Road,
Waitaki, Otago
Ph: (03) 436 0089
www.sublimewine.co.nz

Two Paddocks PAGE 60
PO Box 369, Queenstown,
Central Otago
Ph: (03) 449 2756
www.twopaddocks.com

van Asch Winery PAGE 135
Rapid 1693, SHW 6, Gibbston,
Queenstown, Central Otago
Ph: (03) 442 7310
www.vanaschwines.com

Waitiri Creek Wines PAGE 154
Church Lane, SH6
Gibbston Valley, Central Otago
Ph: (03) 441 3315
www.waitiricreek.co.nz

William Hill Vineyard PAGE 182
Dunstan Road, RD1
Alexandra, Central Otago
Ph: (03) 448 8436
www.williamhill.co.nz

Zebra NZ Vineyards
PAGES 164–166
Rapid 140, Bendigo Loop Road,
RD3, Cromwell, Central Otago
Ph: (03) 445 2060
www.zebranz.com